George Wither

Juvenilia

Poems. Part II

George Wither

Juvenilia
Poems. Part II

ISBN/EAN: 9783744710589

Printed in Europe, USA, Canada, Australia, Japan

Cover: Foto ©Thomas Meinert / pixelio.de

More available books at **www.hansebooks.com**

Publications of the Spenser Society
Issue No. 10

JUVENILIA

POEMS

BY
GEORGE WITHER

CONTAINED IN THE COLLECTIONS OF HIS
JUVENILIA WHICH APPEARED IN
1626 AND 1633

PART II

PRINTED FOR THE SPENSER SOCIETY
1871

THE SCOVRGE.

If thou perceiue fome, as fome will doe then,
Keepe out a many worthy Gentlemen,
And let a Laundreffe or a Scoundrell paffe,
Giue him a ierke, and tell him hee's an Affe.
  But left thou fpy what may make thee afham'd,
(Or fpeake of that for which thou maift be blam'd)
Leaue thou the Court, if thine owne felfe thou pitty,
And come a while to walke about the City.
As foone, as there thou entreft, thou fhalt meet
Great ftore of Gallants pafing out the ftreet.
A part, from Dice, or Fence, or Dancing come,
And peraduenture, from a whore-houfe fome:
Thefe, are good fellowes that will frankly fpend,
While Lands doe laft, or any man will lend;
And yet to fee (more fooles the world had neuer)
They are fo proud, as if 'twould laft for euer.
And though thefe lightly cannot haue a worfe,
Or deadlier fickeneffe, than an empty purfe,
Which will enfue; yet tell them, they muft meet,
At the Kings-bench, the Counters, or the Fleet.
  Then, ftep vnto the Lawyers: peraduenture
They'l by fome *Writ* command thee not to enter.
Yet feare them not; but looke and thou fhalt fpy
Vnder their gownes, a maffe of knauery.
Pluck off the maske of Law, that cloaks their drifts,
And thou fhalt fee a world of lawleffe fhifts.
But, tell them there's a Iudge will not be feed:
And that perhaps will make their Confcience bleed.
  Then tell the Scriueners as thou paffeft by,
That they were beft to leaue their forgery,

THE SCOVRGE.

Or elfe, why is't their eares doe fcape fo well?
The Diuell meanes to beare them whole, to hell.
 Tell the Phyficians (if thou meet with any)
Their Potions and their Drugs haue murther'd many,
For which, thou wouldft haue lafht, but doft delay them,
Becaufe the Diuell meanes to pay them:
But if they'l prooue conclufions, bid them then,
Try't on themfelues, and not on other men.
 Defire the Brokers that they would not yawne
After the forfeit of anothers pawne.
It is their right by Law they'l fay, 'tis true;
And fo's their foule, perhaps, anothers due:
But fting them; if their confcience quite be fled,
Then fhall they pay, what they haue forfeited.
 Entreat the Taylor next, if that he can,
To leaue his theft, and proue an honeft man.
And if he thinke the matter be too hard,
Knocke him about the Noddle with his yard.
If he be rich and take the fame in fnuffe,
Tell him his fubftance is but ftollen ftuffe:
And, that the Iay would hardly brooke the weather,
If euery Bird fhould take away her feather.
So hauing whipt him; let the Prieft goe fhriue him
And (if he haue authoritie) forgiue him.
 Go warne the Crafts-man that he doe not lurke
All day at Ale-houfe, and neglect his worke:
And then furuey the ware of euery Trade,
For much (I tell thee) is deceitfull made.
Which if thou find; I charge thee do not friend it,
But call him knaue, and bid him go and mend it.

Oh

THE SCOVRGE.

Oh fee, if thou the Marchant-man canſt finde,
For heele be gone at turning of the winde :
Bid him keepe touch, or tell his worſhip how
His heart will tremble when the Seas are rough :
Deſire him too, if he doe trauell thither
Where Confcience is, that he would bring fome hither ;
Here's little, fome will haue it ; if none will,
He ſhall gaine by it, though he keepe it ſtill :
If he bring none, 'twere charity I thinke,
To pray fome ſtorme may make his veſſell ſinke.
   Looke in their ſhips, for I haue knowne deceit
Hath been in both the owner, and the fraight ;
Yea, note them well, and thou ſhalt find their books
Are Woodcocks ginnes, and barbed fiſhing hooks :
But he thereby great ſtore of wealth obtaines,
And cares not how, fo he encreafe his gaines :
Yet, leaſt his riches hap to make him proud,
Satyr, I pray thee, tell him this aloud
To make him fmart ; *that, whilſt he like a mome,*
Playes faſt abroad, his wife playes looſe at home :
Nor ſhall his ill-got maſſe of wealth hold out,
But he, or his, become a banquerout.
   Now to thy reſt, 'tis night. But here approaches
A troope with Torches, hurried in their Coaches.
Stay and behold, what are they ? I can tell,
Some bound for Shorditch, or for Clarken-well :
Oh thefe are they which thinke that Fornication,
Is but a youthfull, fportfull, recreation *:*
Thefe to hold out the game, maintaine the backe
With Marrow-Pies, Potato-roots, and Sacke :

                                      And

THE SCOVRGE.

And when that Nature hath confum'd her part,
Can hold out a Luxurious courfe by Art:
Goe, ftop the horfes quickely (leaft thou miffe)
And tell the Coachmans wanton carriage this,
They of their guide muft be aduifed well,
For they are running downe the hill to hell.
Their Venery, will foone confume their ftocks,
And bring them to repentance with a pocks.

For other crimes committed without light,
Let fuch reueale as fee like Owles by night:
For many men a fecret fault can finde,
But in apparant roageries are blinde.
Or elfe, they will not fee; but thou wert beft
Leaue whipping, and betake thee to thy reft.
If in an Inne it be, before thou fup,
Will that the Tapfter call his Mafter vp,
And bid him kindly, fith there lodge thou muft
To vfe plaine-dealing like an honeft Hoft.
Diffembling's nought, hard reckonings they are worfe;
Light gaines (they fay) *will make a heauy purfe.*
And let him not (a fault with many rife)
For bafe aduantage proftitute his wife;
For many men (who are not what they fhould be)
Do make their wiues more wanton than they would be.
Thereby they gaine, their Innes are ill frequented;
But fuch ill courfes are too late repented.
So fchoole him well, but, doe thy whip refraine,
And fend him to his other guefts againe.

Then thou fhalt fee the nimble Tapfter fly,
Still yauling, *Here, anon fir, by and by.*

So

THE SCOVRGE.

So diligent that time, more knowne muſt make him,
Or, for an honeſt man thou wilt miſtake him;
His beſt reuenue is by *Nicke* and *Froth*;
Which priuiledge to loofe, they would be loth.
And, there's an old ſhift (if they leaue it not)
There muſt be ſomething added to the ſhot.
But wilt thou ſwagger with him for it? No:
But take him as he is, and let him goe.
 Now for moſt Hoſtlers if you hap to try them,
Knaues thou maiſt ſay they are, and not belie them;
For, they deceiue the poore dumbe trauelling beaſt,
And for the fame deſerue a ierke at leaſt;
Yet, doe thou ſpare them: for there is no doubt,
Some gueſt will find a time to pay the lout.
 Well, hauing reſted, and difcharg'd thine Hoſt,
Ile ſend thee downe into the Country, Poſt:
For I haue buſineſſe, no man would belieue,
With whom d'ye thinke? e'ne with the vnder-Shrieue:
Tell him thou heardſt (and that's a fault indeed)
That in ſome cauſes he is double-feed.
And that moreouer he deſerues a portion
With thoſe that are indited for extortion;
Yea and for other things as well as that,
Tell him the countrey termes him, he knowes what.
Whereat if thou perceiue, he make a ſport
Thou whip him ſhalt, till he be ſorry for't.
Say to our Knights; their much formality,
Hath made them leaue their Hoſpitality:
And ſay (although they angry, be therefore)
That many of themſelues ar'not onely poore,

Y 3   But

THE SCOVRGE.

But that they haue to (or they are belied)
Quite begger'd their pofterity with pride.
    And fith thou art fo neere them ; doe not ceafe
Vntill thou fee our Iuftices of Peace :
There, try if thou canft get but fo much fauour,
To binde the Country to the good behauiour.
And tell them, how, thou haft enformed beene,
That they haue granted Warrants vpon fpleene ;
Are partiall, and haue ouer-fway'd by might
The poore mans caufe that's innocent and right :
If this thou finde be true, thou haft permiffion
To lafh, or put them out of the Commiffion.
    The Conftable, if he were bid, I wiffe,
Be good in's office, 'twere not much amiffe :
For he, they fay, a many meanes may haue
If fo he be difpos'd to play the knaue ;
See how he deales, and make thy meffage knowne,
For he hath ftocks, and whipping-pofts of 's owne.
    There are Church-wardens too, I fhame to fee
How they runne into wilfull periurie.
Partly in fauour, and in part for feare,
They winke at much diforder in a yeare :
But if thou hap to take them in the lurch,
Ierke them, as euill members of the Church.
If they reply, offenders are fo friended
Though they prefent, 'tis little thing amended :
Yet tell them 'tis their dutie to difcharge
Their confciences in euery thing at large ;
Which if they doe, ill dooers fhall be fham'd,
Or the corrupted Vifitors be blam'd.
                                        And

THE SCOVRGE.

And prethee tell the B. Chancellors
That thou art fent to be their counfellors :
And will them, if they meane not to be ftript,
And to be once againe like fchoole-boyes whipt
Their worfhips would not fo corrupted be ;
To hinder Iuftice for a fcuruy fee.
    Then next goe tell their reuerend good Mafters,
That thou and they are like to fall to wafters :
Faith ; thou fhalt finde their Doctorfhips, perhaps,
Difputing of their Surpleffes and Caps,
About the holy Croffe, a Gowne, a Hood,
Or fome fuch matter for the Churches good :
But tell them, there are other things to do,
A great deale fitter to be lookt into ;
And if they pleafe to goe their Vifitation,
There's waightier matters looke for reformation.
Yea, fay there's many an infirmity
Which they both may, and ought to remedy :
But touch them with remembrance of their place,
And they perhaps will alter then the cafe.
    Then bid thofe Dunces in our Colledges,
That they prouide them good Apologies ;
For 'tis reported lately, they haue both
Betooke themfelues to venery, and floth,
And feeke not learning onely, as they fhould,
But are back-friends to many a man that would :
'Twere fit they made a publique recantation,
And were well whipt before a Congregation.
    So leauing them their wits for to refine,
Thou fhalt be bold to looke on the Diuine ;

THE SCOVRGE.

They fay he's growne more carefull of his ftocke,
Of profits and of tithes, than of his flocke:
Now if thou finde report hath not beli'd him,
With good refpect vnto his Calling, chide him.
  I had almoft forgot our ciuill Doctors;
I pray thee warne them and their lazie Proctors,
They would not vfe to make fo many paufes,
Before they doe determine poore mens caufes,
And let them not fuppofe their fees are fmall,
Sith they at laft will get the Diuell and all.
  There be Court-Barons, many in thy way,
Thus maift thou to the Steward of them fay;
Their policiy in raifing fines and rents,
Hath put poore men befides their Tenements:
And tell them (let them anfwer if they can)
Their falfe Court-roles haue vndone many a man.
Say thou haft feene what to their place belong'd,
And knowft oft-times both Lord and Tenants wrong'd:
Yet fpare thy whip; for why? the peoples curfe
Already hath prepared them a worfe.
  So when thou thus haft punifht Vices flaues,
And roundly ierkt the Country petty knaues,
Then march thou to the Campe, and tell thou, there
The lufty ruffling, fhuffling Caualere,
(Whofe hardned heart can brooke to rob and fpill
His friend or foe; to ruine, wound or kill)
That he will one day finde a mifery
Will dog him to reuenge his cruelty:
And fee that thou the Ruffians courage quaile,
Or lafh him, till the ftocke and whip-cord faile.
                                    Walke

THE SCOVRGE.

Walke but the Round, and thou maift hap to catch
The careleffe Souldiers fleeping in their watch;
Or in a march perhaps they'l goe aftray:
But, if thou fee them out of their array,
And without leaue and warrant roming out,
To fetch fome defperate booty there about,
Remember them; and for their ftout brauado's,
See thou reward them with found baftinado's.
Then bid the Captaines in their Garifons,
Not lay to pawne their rich Caparifons,
Nor runne vpon the fcore till they are forc't
To be difarm'd for payment, or vnhors't,
Nor keepe the Souldiers hire, left they be faine
To make an infurrection, or complaine.
For, that indeed, proues oftentimes the caufe
They doe fo much tranfgreffe the Martiall lawes.
Yea, tell them tis a fcandall to be drunke,
And drown their valour; or maintaine a Punke.
Then if they mend it not, to blot their fame,
In fteed of honour, whip them for't with fhame.

Laftly, there are fome felfe-conceited wits,
Whofe ftomacks nought but their owne humor fits;
Detracting Critriks; who e'ne at the beft,
Doe bite with enuy, or elfe fnarle at leaft:
And in thy Progreffe if difcern'd thou be,
'Tis out of queftion they will fnap at thee.
To fpight them then, the waie's not to out-brawle them:
But fay thou car'ft not, and that lafh will gaule them.

Now *Satyr*, leaue me to my felfe alone;
Thou haft thy meffage, and thou maift be gone:

Whip

THE SCOVRGE.

Whip any that fhall offer to withftand thee
In executing that which I command thee.
 And yet, (*fo ho, ho, ho,*) come backe againe,
Be fure that thou doe vnderftand me plaine.
Firft note ; I from my Scourge doe here except
The Guard by whom the Kingdomes peace is kept,
The vertuous Peeres; know, that I nothing grutch them :
And on my bleffing fee thou doe not touch them.
 And, if in all our Offices there's any
That is an honeft man, among fo many,
Him did I euer meane that thou fhould'ft fpare ;
Becaufe I know that fuch an one is rare.
 Phyficke and Law I honour (as tis fit,)
With euery vertuous man profeffing it ;
I doe not ayme at fuch as they : Nor when
I flout our Gallants, meane I Gentlemen,
That well and decently maintained be
According to their fafhion and degree :
No, thofe I loue ; and what can I leffe doe,
Sith I of them am well-beloued too ?
 To blame all Marchants, neuer was my will ;
Nor doe I thinke all Trades-mens worke is ill :
My meaning muft not fo be vnderftood ;
For the laft fhooes I had were very good.
 Yea, and fo farre am I from fuch a thought
Thou fhould'ft againft the Vertuous doe ought :
That if thou but an honeft Tapfter fee,
Tell him I wifh we might acquainted be ;
And Ile that Hoftler loue, which in amends
Will vfe my horfe well, that we may be friends.
            And

323

THE SCOVRGE.

And to be briefe, Good *Satyr* vnderstand,
That thou maist not mistake what I command:
'Tis not my meaning, neither doe I like
That thou at this time should'st in speciall strike:
Becaufe my hatred might appeare as then,
Not to the vice, but rather to the men.
Which is not fo ; for though fome malice me,
With euery one I am in charity.
   And if that thou doe euer come to fight,
And bring thy yet concealed charge to light ;
I wish it might be tooke as 'twas intended,
And then no vertuous man will be offended.
But, if that any man will thinke amis,
Vpon my life that party guilty is :
And therefore lash him. So, get th'out of dore ;
Come what come will, Ile call thee backe no more.
   Well now he's gone the way that I direct him,
And goe he shall how ere the world refpect him :
If any meruaile why he was not bolder,
Perhaps he may be when that he is older :
He hath too fmooth a chin, a looke too milde,
A token that he is not wholly wilde ;
But may I reach the yeeres of other men,
If this loofe world be not amended then,
I'le fend a *Satyr* rougher than a Beare,
That shall not chide & whip, but fcratch and teare ;
And fo I'le teach him, he shall be too strong.
For all your *Paris-garden dogs* to wrong.
This *Satyr* hath a Scourge, (but it wants weight :
Your *Spanish* whips were worfe in eighty-eight)
                                            That

THE SCOVRGE.

That, fhall not onely make them howle for paine,
But toufe them, till they hold their peace againe.
   Now, if the world doe frowne vpon me for't :
Shall I be forry ? No, 'twill mend my fport ;
But what if I my felfe fhould hap to ftray
Out of my bounds, into my *Satyrs* way ?
Why then ; (and that's as much as I need doo)
I'le giue him leaue to come and lafh me too.
   So now my *Mufe* a refting time requires
For fhee's o'rewearied, and her Spirit tires.

Πάντοτε δόξα Θεῷ.

FINIS.

Certaine Epigrams to the *Kings*
moſt excellent Maieſty, the Queene, the
Prince, the Princeſſe, and other Noble
and Honourable Perſonages, and
Friends, to whom the Author
gaue any of his Books.

To the Kings Maieſtie.

EPIGRAM. I.

Loe *here dread* Sou'raign, *and great* Britaines *King,*
Firſt, to thy view, I haue preſum'd to bring
Theſe my Eſſaies ; *On which but gently looke,*
I doe not make thee Patron of my Booke ;
For, 'tis not fit our Faiths-Defender (*ſtill*)
Take the protection of each trifling quill.
No, yet becauſe thy wiſedome able is
Of all things to make vſe ; *I giue thee this* :
The Picture *of a beaſt in* Humane *ſhape* ;
Tis neither Monkey, *nor* Baboone, *nor* Ape,
Though necre condition'd. I haue not ſought it
In Affrick *Deſerts, neither haue I brought it*
Out of Ignota terrà, *thoſe wilde Lands*
Beyond the fartheſt Megalanick *ſtrands*
                                                                Yeeld

EPIGRAMS.

Yeeld not the like; the Fiend liues in this Ile,
And I much mus'd thou ſpi'dſt not all this while
That man-like Monſter. But (alas!) I ſaw,
The looke of Maieſty kept him in awe:
He will not, (for he dares not) before thee
Shew what (indeed) it is his vſe to be.
But, in thy preſence he is meeke, demure
Deuout, chaſte, honeſt, innocent, and pure:
(Seeming an Angel, free from thought of ill,)
And therefore, thou muſt needs ſo thinke him ſtill.
 But, for becauſe thy Soueraigne place denies
The ſight of what is view'd by meaner eyes,
This I haue brought thee with much care and paine:
'Twas like to haue beene forcèd backe againe.
So loath the world was, that thine eye ſhould view
The Portraiture that I haue drawne ſo true:
Yea, yet (I feare) ſhe findes her ſelfe ſo gall'd,
That ſome will ſtudie how to hau't recall'd:
But tis too late; for now my Muſe doth truſt,
When thou haſt ſeen't, thou wilt approue what's iuſt.
 And if I may but once perceiue, or heare,
That this ſound's pleaſing in thy Kingly eare,
Ile make my Muſes to deſcribe him fuller,
And paint him foorth in a more liuely colour.
Yea I will to the worlds great ſhame vnfold
That which is knowne, but neuer yet was told.
  Mean-while, great King, a happy Monarch raigne,
  In ſpight of Rome, the Diuell, Hell, and Spaine.

            Another

Another to his Maieftie.

EPIGRAM. 2.

<blockquote>

AS hee that feeds on no worfe meat than Quailes,
And with choife dainties pleafeth Appetite,
Will neuer haue great lift to gnaw his nailes,
Or in a courfe thin diet take delight:
So thou great KING that ftill doft ouer-looke
    The learned works that are moft deep, moft rare,
Canft not perhaps my ruder Satyrs brooke,
    Nor doft thou for fuch fharp-fangd Criticks care.
Oh doe not yet thy felfe fo much eftrange
    From wonted curtefie to others fhowne,
A Countrie difh doth often ferue for change;
    And fomething here is worthie to be knowne.
Sharpe fauce giues fweeteft meat a better tafte,
    And though that this to many bitter be,
Thou no fuch fickneffe in thy ftomacke haft,
    And therefore 'twill be pleafing vnto thee.
What, though I neither flatter, fawne, nor footh,
    My honeft plaineneffe fhall more truly praife thee,
Than thofe that in Court-language filed fmooth,
    Striue vnbeleeued Tropheis for to raife thee,
                               My

</blockquote>

EPIGRAMS.

My loyall heart cannot ſo well impart
 The loue it beares your Maiesty *as others* :
 The want of Time, Encouragement, *and* Art,
 My purpoſe in the Embrio *ſtill ſmothers.*
Obſcuritie, croſſe-Fates, *and want of* Meanes,
Would haue made Rome's *great* Maro *harſhly ſing :*
 But if once Cæſar *to his Muſicke leanes,*
 His tunes through all the world will ſweetly ring.
And this made Engliſh wits, late famous growne,
 Eliz'as *princely hand did oft peruſe,*
 Their well tun'd Poems ; *and her bounty ſhowne ?*
And that giues light and life to euery Muſe.
Oh! *had I ſuch a* Star *for* Pole *to mine,*
I'de reach a Straine ſhould rauiſh all the Nine.

To the Queenes Maieſtie.

EPIGRAM. 3.

In poſſe.

D*Aughter, Wife, Siſter, Mother to a King.*
 And Empreſſe of the North, enrich thy Name ;
  Yet thou doſt chaſtitie and wiſedome bring
  Bountie, and Bounty to make vp thy fame.
Which ſith (faire Queene) *my* Muſe *hath vnderſtood,*
She's bold into thy preſence to intrude ;

Aſſured

EPIGRMS.

*Assured, honest meanings that are good
Shall finde acceptance there, though they seeme rude.*
 Looke and behold the Vanities *of Men,
 Their* Miseries, *their* Weaknesses *and* Pride;
 *And when described by my rurall Pen,
 Thou each particular hast here espide,
Thinke with thyselfe how blest thy Fortunes be,
T'enioy so rare a Prince, that both knowes how
To keepe himselfe from such fell* Passion *free,
And make so many mad-wilde creatures bow :*
 Indeed heere's Vices *tablet plainely made,
 Not veiled ouer, or obscurely drawne;
 'Tis in a colour which shall neuer fade,
 That men may blush on such a Hag to fawne.
But if your* Grace *will fauour what I sing,
Though* Vertue *be in durance, Ile repreeue her,
That-now despised-*Nymph *to honour bring,
Set all her hidden beauties forth ; and giue her*
 *So sweet a looke, and such a deft attire,
 Men shall grow loue-sicke, and burne with desire,*

To CHARLES, Prince of Wales

EPIGRAM. 4.

SEe heere, faire *Offspring* of the Royall *Ste*
What all the world almost is subiect to;

EPIGRAMS.

Behold it fo, thou truely mayft contemne,
And from thy heart abhorre, what others doe ;
Now is the fit and onely time to feafon
That yong rare-vnderftanding breaft of thine
With *facred precepts, good aduice,* and *reafon.*
But there's no doubt thou wilt to good incline :
Inheritance great Prince will make it thine.
  And were *Mans* nature yet more prone to fall,
  So to be borne, and taught, would helpe it all.

To the Princeffe.

EPIGRAM. 5.

SWeet *Princeffe*; tho my *Mufe* fing not the glories
 Of faire aduent'rous Knights, or Ladies loues :
Though here be no *Encomiafticke* ftories,
 That tender hearts, to gentle pitty moues :
Yet in an honeft homely Rufticke ftraine,
She limmes fuch creatures, as may you nere know.
Forgiue her, though fhe be feuere or plaine
Truth, that may warrant it, commanded fo.
 Yea, view it ouer with beliefe, but than,
 I am afraid you will abhorre a man.

 And yet you need not ; All deferue not blame,
 For that great *Prince* that wooeth to be yours,
            If

EPIGRAMS.

(If that his worth but equalize his fame,)
Is free from any *Satyr* here of ours.
Nay, they fhal praife him ; for though they haue whips
To make the wicked their offences rue,
And dare to fcourge the greateft when he trips,
Vertue fhall ftill be certaine of her due.
But for your fake (if that you entertaine him)
Oh would he were a man as I could faine him.

Yet fweet *Elizabeth* : that happy name,
If we loft nothing elfe by lofing thee,
So deare to *England* is, we are to blame
If without teares and fighes we parted be :
But if thou muft make bleft another Clime ;
Remember *Our* : and for that though I vfe
A crabbed fubiect and a churlifh rime,
Deigne but to be the Miftris of my *Mufe* ;
And I'le change *Theames*, and in a lofty ftile,
Keepe thee aliue for euer in this *Ile*.

To the Lords of his Maiefties moft Honourable *Priuie Councell*.

EPIGRAM. 6

M *Oft honour'd Lords* ; I here prefent this book,
To your graue Cenfures, not to fhew my *Art* :

332
EPIGRAMS.

Nere did you on fo rude a matter looke,
    Yet, 'tis the token of an honeft heart.
I did it not to pleafe or flatter any,
    Nor haue I made it for the thirft of gaine;
For I am fure it will not humour many,
    And I expeft much hatred for my paine.
Here, fomething you may fee, that now requires
    Your care and prouidence to haue't amended:
That is, the height to which my *Mufe* afpires,
    And whereto I haue all my labour tended.
It may be, there be fome, out of their hate,
    Will mif-interpret what is plainely meant;
Or taxe me as too fawcy with the *State*,
    In hope to make me for the truth be fhent:
Yet know *Great Lords*, I doe acknowledge here,
    It is your *Wifedomes*, that next God maintaines
This Kingdomes good; And from my heart I beare
    A reuerent refpeft vnto your paines.
I doe not, as fuch faine would haue it feeme,
    Prefume to teach your Wifedomes what is beft;
I doe not mine owne knowledge fo efteeme:
    Vile felfe-conceit I *(* from my heart*)* deteft.
But for becaufe I know the piercingft eye
    Can neuer into all abufes fee:
And fith the greateft in authoritie
    May not behold fometime fo much as we:
What therefore I haue thought to be amiffe,
    And worth amending I haue told it here:
I know your Hononrs will be pleas'd in this,
    Though fome (it may be) cannot rage forbeare:
                                                    But

EPIGRAMS:

But if there's any take this writing badly,
Had it told all, it would haue vext him madly.

To HENRY, Earle of *Southhampton.*

EPIGRAM. 7.

SOuth-hampton; fith thy *Prouince* brought me forth,
And on thofe pleafant Mountaines I yet keepe,
I ought to be no ftranger to thy worth,
Nor let thy Vertues in obliuion fleepe.
Nor will I, if my fortunes giue me time:
Meane while read this, and fee what others be.
If thou canft like't, and wil't but grace my Rime,
I will fo blaze thy *Hampfhire* Springs and *Thee,*
Thy *Arle, Teft, Stowre,* and *Auon* fhall fhare *Fame,*
Either with *Humber, Seuerne, Trent,* or *Thame.*

To WILLIAM, Earle of *Pembroke.*

EPIGRAM. 8.

THou whom no priuate endes can make vniuft,
*(*True Noble Spirit, free from hate or guile*)*

EPIGRAMS.

Thou, whom thy Prince, for thy great care and truſt,
Hath plac't to keepe the entrance of this *Ile*,
See heere th' abuſes of theſe wicked Times:
I haue expoſ'd them open to thy view,
Thy iudgement is not blinded with like crimes,
And therefore maiſt perceiue that all is true.
    Tak't: for though I ſeeme a ſtranger, I know thee;
And for thy vertues (*Penbroke*) this I owe thee.

To the Lord *Liſle*, Lord Chamberlaine
to the Queene.

EPIGRAM. 9.

A *Sidney* being, and ſo neere allied
To him whoſe matchleſſe rare immortall pen
    Procur'd of Fame to haue him deified,
    And liue for euer in the hearts of men:
The loue my ſoule hath euer borne that name,
Would certainely perſwade me for your ſake,
    In honeſt ſeruice to aduenture blame,
    Or any open dangers vndertake:
Yet ſhall not That, your Titles, nor your Place,
Your Honours, nor your Might, nor all you haue,
    Cauſe me to flatter, for regard or grace,
Fortune ſhall neuer make my minde a ſlaue:
But ſeeing that your Vertue ſhines apparant,
And honourable acts doe ſpeake your praiſe:

                                Sith

EPIGRAMS:

Sith *Good report* hath giuen forth her warrant,
 Which none *(*so much as by himselfe*)* gaine-sayes,
That (and nought elfe but that) compels my *Muse*
 To sing your *worth*, and to present her *owne*.
  If this imperfect issue you'l peruse,
 I'le make her in a better forme be knowne,
And teach her, that is now so rude and plaine,
 To soare a pitch aboue the common straine.

To the Lady *Mary Wroth.*

EPIGRAM. 10.

Madame, to call you *best*, or the *most faire*,
 The *vertu'st* and the *wisest* in our dayes:
Is now not commendations worth a haire,
 For that's become to be each huswiues praise.

There's no degree below Superlatiue,
 Will serue some soothing Epigrammatists:
The *Worst* they praise, exceeds Comparatiue,
 And *Best* can get no more out of their fists.

But *Arts sweet Louer* (vnto whom I know,
 There is no happy *Muse* this day remaines,
That doth not to your worth and seruice owe,
 (At least the best and sweetest of his straines,)
Vouch-

EPIGRAMS.

Vouchfafe to let this Booke your fauour finde:
And as I here haue *Mans* abufes fhowne,
Thofe *Mufes* vnto whom you are enclinde,
Shall make your worth and vertues fo well knowne:

While others falfe praife, fhall in one's mouth be,
All, fhall commend you, in the high'ft degree.

To the Lord *Ridgeway*.

EPIGRAM. II.

SIR, you firft grac't and gratifi'd my *Mufe*,
   Which nere durft try till then what fhe could doe:
That which I did, vnto my felfe was newes;
   A matter, I was little vs'd vnto:
Had you thofe firft endeauours not approu'd
   Perhaps I had for euer filence kept;
But now your good encouragement hath moou'd,
   And rous'd my Spirits, that before time flept;
For which, I vow'd a gift that fhould be better:
Accept this for't, and Ile be ftill your debter.

Heere you fhall fee the Images of Men
   More *fauage* than the wildeft *Irifh kerne:*
Abufes whipt and ftript, and whipt agen;
   I know your iudgement can the *Truth* difcerne.
                                        Now

EPIGRAMS.

Now fo you well will thinke of this my Rime,
   I'ue fuch a minde yet to Saint *Patricks* Ile,
That if my Fate and Fortunes giue me time,
   I purpofe to re-uifit you a while,
And make thofe fparks of honour to flame high
That rak't vp in obliuions cinders lie.

To his Father.

EPIGRAM. 12.

OThers may glory, that their Fathers hands
Haue fcrap't together mighty fums of gold,
Boaft in the circuit of new purchaft lands,
Or heards of Cattell more than can be told.
God giue them ioy; their wealth Ile nere enuy,
For you haue gotten me a greater ftore,
And though I haue not their profperitie,
In my conceit I am not halfe fo poore.
You learn't me with a little to content me,
Shew'd how to bridle paffion in fome meafure;
And through your meanes, I haue a *Talent* lent me,
Which I more value than all *Indies* treafure.
For, when the almoft boundleffe Patrimonies
Are wafted; thofe, by which our Great ones truft
To be eterniz'd: when their braueries
Shall be forgotten, and their Tombes be duft;
                              Then

EPIGRAMS.

Then, to the glory of your future line,
Your owne and my friends facred memory,
This little, poore, defpifed *wealth* of mine
Shall raife a *Trophee* of eternitie:
Which fretting *Enuy*, nor confuming *Time*,
Shall ere abolifh or one whit offend:
A topleffe *Statue*, that to Starres fhall climbe,
Such fortune fhall my honeft minde attend.

But I muft needs confeffe, 'tis true, I yet
Reape little profit in the eyes of men.
My Talent yeelds fmall outward benefit,
Yet I'le not leaue it for the world agen.
Though't bring no gaine that you by artfull fleight
Can meafure out the Earth in part or whole;
Sound out the Centers depth, and take the height
Either of th'Artick, or Antartick Pole;
Yet 'tis your pleafure, it contentment brings:
And fo my *Mufe* is my content and ioy:
I would not miffe her to be rankt with Kings,
How-euer fome account it as a toy.

But hauing then (and by your means) obtain'd
So rich a Patrimonie for my fhare,
(For which with links of loue I'me euer chain'd)
What duties fitting for fuch bounties are.

Moreouer, Nature brought me in your debt,
And ftill I owe you for your cares and feares:
Your paines and charges I doe not forget,
Befides the intereft of many yeeres.
What way is there to make requitall for it?
Much I fhall leaue vnpaid doe what I can:

                                      Should

EPIGRAMS.

Should I be then vnthankfull? I abhor it,
The Will may ferue, when Power wants in man.
  This booke I giue you then; here you fhall finde
Somewhat to counteruaile your former coft:
It is a little *Index* of my minde;
Time fpent in reading it will not be loft.
Accept it, and when I haue to my might
Paid all I can to you; if Powers Diuine
Shall fo much in my happineffe delight
To make you Grandfire to a fonne of mine;
    Looke what remaines, and may by right be due,
    Ile pay it him, as 'twas receiu'd from you.

Your louing Sonne
George Wither.

To his Mother.

EPIGRAM. 13.

VNgratefull is the childe that can forget
  The Mothers many paines, her cares, her feares,
And therefore, though I cannot pay the debt
Due for the fmalleft drop of your kinde teares;
This Booke I for acknowledgement doe giue you,
Wherein you may perceiue my heart and minde;
Let neuer falfe report of me more grieue you,
And you fhall fure no iuft occafion finde

Loue

EPIGRAMS.

Loue made you apt to feare thofe flanders true,
Which in my abfence were but lately fowne ;
It was a motherly diftruft in you,
But thofe that rais'd them are falfe villaines knowne.
For though I muft confeffe I am indeed
The vileft to my felfe that liues this time ;
Yet to the world-ward I haue tane fuch heed,
There's none can fpot me with a haynous crime.
  This I am forc't to fpeake, you beft know why :
  And I dare ftrike him that dare fay I lye ?

To his deere Friend, Mafter
Thomas Cranly.

EPIGRAM. 14.

BRother, for fo I call thee, not becaufe
Thou wert my Fathers or my Mothers fonne ;
Not confanguinity, nor wedlocke lawes
Could fuch a kindred twixt vs haue begunne :
  We are not of one bloud, nor yet name neither,
  Nor fworn in brother-hood with alehoufe quarts,
  We neuer were fo much as drunke together :
'Twas no fuch flight acquaintance ioyn'd our harts,
But a long knowledge with much triall did it ;
(Which are to chufe a friend the beft directions.)
And though we lou'd both well at firft, both hid it,
Till 'twas difcouer'd by alike affections,
                                    Since

EPIGRAMS.

Since which, thou haſt o're-gone me far in ſhewing
The office of a Friend. Doe ſo and ſpare not:
*(*Lo, here's a *Memorandum* for what's owing;*)*
But, know, for all thy kinde reſpect I care not,
Vnleſſe thoul't ſhow how I may ſeruice doe thee:
Then will I ſweare I am beholding to thee.

Thine, G. W.

To his louing Friend and Couſen-German, Mr. *William Wither*.

EPIGRAM. 15.

IF that the *Standerds* of the houſe bewray
What *Fortunes* to the owners may betide;
Or if their Deſtinies, as ſome men ſay,
Be in the names of any ſignifi'd,
Tis ſo in thine: for that faire antique *Shield*,
Borne by thy Predeceſſors long agoe,
Depainted with a cleare pure *Argent* field,
The innocencie of thy line did ſhow.
Three ſable Creſents with a Cheueron gul'd,
Tels that blacke *Fates* obſcur'd our houſes light;
Becauſe the *Planet* that our fortunes rul'd,
Loſt her owne luſtre, and was darkned quite:

And

EPIGRAMS.

And, as indeed our Aduerfaries fay,
    The very name of *Wither* fhowes decay:
But yet defpaire not, keepe thy *White* vnftain'd,
And then it skils not what thy *Crefcents* be.
What though the *Moone* be now increaft, now wan'd?
Learne thence to know thy lifes inconftancie;
Be carefull as thou hitherto haft bin,
To fhun th' Abufes *Man* is taxt for here:
And then that brightneffe now eclipft with fin,
When *Moone* and *Sun* are darkned, fhall looke cleare:
And what fo e're thy name may feeme to threat,
That quality braue things doth promife thee;
Ere thou fhalt want, thy *Hare* will bring thee meat,
And to kill care, her felfe thy make-fport be:
    Yea, (though yet *Enuies* mifts do make them dull)
    I hope to fee the waned *Orbes* at full.

EPIGRAMS.

To his Schoole-Mafter, Mafter
Iohn Greaues.

EPIGRAM. 16.

IF euer I doe wifh I may be rich
(As oft perhaps fuch idle breath I fpend)
   I doe it not for any thing fo much
   As to haue wherewithall to pay my Friend.
For, (truft me) there is nothing grieues me more
Than this ; that I fhould ftill much kindneffe take,
   And haue a fortune (to my minde) fo poore,
   That (though I would) amends I cannot make :
Yet, to be ftill as thankfull as I may ;
(Sith my eftate no better meanes affords.)
   What I in deeds receiue, I doe repay
   In willingnes, in thanks, and gentle words.
Then though your loue doth well deferue to haue
Better requitals than are in my power ;
   Knowing you'l nothing *vltra poſſe* craue
   Here I haue brought you thefe *Eſſaies* of our.
You may thinke much (perhaps) fith there's fo many
Learn'd *Graduats* that haue your *Pupils* been ;
   I, who am none, and more vnfit than any,
   Should firft prefume in publicke to be feene :
But you haue heard thofe horfes in the teem
That with their worke are ableft to goe through,
                            So

EPIGRAMS.

So forward feldome as blinde *Bayard* feeme,
Or giue fo many twitches to the plough :
And fo though they may better ; their intent
Is not, perhaps, to foole themfelues in print.

To the captious Reader.

WHat thou maift fay or think now tis no matter :
   But if thou bufily imagine here,
Sith moft of thefe are great ones, that I flatter ;
Know, facred *Iuftice* is to me fo deare,
  Did not their *vertues* in my thoughts thus raife them,
  To get an *Empire* by them, I'de not praife them.

FINIS.

PRINCE HENRIES
OBSEQVIES;
Or
MOVRNEFVLL ELEGIES
vpon his Death:

With

A suppofed Inter-locution betweene
the Ghoft of Prince *Henry*, and
Great Britaine.

By GEORGE WITHER.

LONDON,
Printed by *T. S.* for *Iohn Budge*, dwelling in Pauls-
Church-yard at the Signe of the Greene
Dragon. 1 6 2 2.

TO THE RIGHT HONOV-
rable, *Robert* Lord *Sidney* of *Penshurſt*,
Vicount *Liſley*, Lord Chamberlaine to the
Queenes Maieſty, & L. Gouernour of
Vluſhing, and the Caſtle of *Ramekins*.

GEORGE WITHER preſents theſe Elegiak-
ſonnets, and wiſheth double Comfort after his
two-fold ſorrow.

Anagramms on the name of Sir *William*
Sidney Knight, deceaſed.

Gulielmus Sidneius.
En vilis, gelidus ſum.
* But *
Ei' nil luge, ſidus ſum.

B*Eſide our great and* Vniuerſall *care,*
(Wherein you one of our chiefe ſharers are)
To adde more grieſe *vnto your* grieſes *begun,*
Whilſt we a Father *loſt, you loſt a* Son,
Whoſe hapleſſe want had more apparant beene,
But darkened by the Other *'twas vnſeene,*

The Epistle.

Which well perceiuing, loth indeed was I,
The Memory *of one fo deare fhould die :*
Occafion thereupon, I therefrre tooke
Thus to prefent your honour with this Booke,
(Vnfained, and true mournefull Elegies,
And for our H E N R Y, my laft Obfequies*)*
That he, which did your Sonnes *late death obfcure,*
Might be the Meane *to make his fame endure :*
But, this may but renew your former woe :
Indeed and I might well haue doubted fo,
Had not I knowne, that Vertue, *which did place you*
Aboue the common fort did alfo grace you ;
With gifts of Minde, *to make you more excell,*
And farre more able, Paffions *rage to quell.*
You can, and may with moderation moane,
For all your comfort is not loft with one :
Children you haue, whofe Vertues *may renew*
The comfort of decaying Hopes *in you.*
Praifed be God, for fuch great bleffings giuing,
And happy you, to haue fuch comforts liuing.
Nor doe I thinke it can be rightly fcd,
You are vnhappy in this One *that's dead :*
For notwithftanding his firft Anagram
Frights, with *Behold, now cold, and vile I am :
Yet in his laft, he feemes more cheerefull farre,
And ioyes, with *Soft, mourne not, I am a Starre.

* The Eng-
lifh of this *Oh great preferment : what could he afpire*
Anagram. *That was more high, or you could more defire?*
Well, fince his foule in heau'n fuch glory hath,
My Loue *bequeathes his* Graue, *this* Epitaph.

Here

Dedicatorie.

EPITAPH.
Heere vnder lies a S I D N E Y : And what than ?
Dooſt thinke heere lies but reliques of a man ?
Know ; 'tis a Cabanet did once include
Wit, Beauty, Sweetnes, Court'ſie, Fortitude.

So let him reſt, to Memory *ſtill deare,*
Till his Redeemer *in the Clowdes appeare.*
Meane while ; *accept his* Will, *who meaning plaine,*
Doth neither write for Praiſe, nor hope of Gaine :
And now your Teares, *and priuate* Griefe, *forbeare,*
To turne vnto our Great *and* Publique Care.

Your Honours true honorer,
George Wither.

351

To the whole world in generall, and more
particularly to the Iles of great *Britaine* and *Ireland*, &c.

Big-fwolne with fighes, and almoft drown'd in teares
My *Mufe* out of a dying trance vp-reares ;
Who yet not able to expreffe her moanes,
*(*Infteed of better vtterance) here, groanes.
And left my clofe-breaft fhould her health impaire,
Is thus amongft you come to take the ayre.
I need not name the griefes that on her feaze,
Th'are known by this, beyond th'*Antipodes*.
But to your view fome heauy rounds fhe brings,
That you may beare the burthen, when fhe fings :
And that's but *Woe* : which you fo high fhould ftraine,
That heauens high vault might Eccho't backe againe.
Then, though I haue not ftriued to feeme witty,
Yet read, and reading note, and noting pitty.
What though there's others, fhow in this more Art ?
I haue as true ; as forrowfull a heart :
What though *Opinion* giue me not a *Name*,
And I was ne're beholding yet to *Fame* ?
Fate would *(*perhaps) my *Mufe*, as yet vnknowne,
Should firft in *Sorrowes* liuery be fhowne.
Then, be the witneffe of my difcontent,
And fee, if griefes haue made me Eloquent :
For here I mourne, for your-our publique loffe ;
And doe my pennance, at the *Weeping Croffe*.

The moft forrowfull,
G. W.

D*Eath* (that by ſtealth did wound *Prince H.* hart)
Is now tane Captiue, and doth act the part
Of one o'recome, by being too too fierce,
And lies himſelfe dead vnder *Henries* hearſe :
    He therefore now in heauenly tunes doth Sing,
    Hell, where's thy triumph ? Death where is thy Sting?

PRINCE *HENRIES* *Obsequies*;

OR

Mournefull Elegies vpon his death:

With

A supposed Inter-locution betweene the Ghost of Prince *Henry*, and Great *Britaine*.

Eleg. 1.

NOw that beloued *Henries* glasse is runne,
And others duties to his body showne;
Now, that his sad-sad *Obsequies* be done,
And publique sorrowes well-nigh ouer-blowne:
Now giue me leaue to leaue all Ioyes at one,
For a dull Melancholy lonelinesse;
To pine my selfe with a selfe-pining mone,
And fat my griefe with solitarinesse
For, if it be a comfort in distresse,
(As some thinke) to haue sharers in our woes,
Then my desire is to be comfortlesse.
(My Soule in publique griefe no pleasure knowes.)
   Yea, I could wish, and for that wish would die,
   That there were none had cause to grieue but I.

For

Prince Henries *Obsequies.*

Eleg. 2.

For were there none had caufe to grieue but I,
'Twould from my *Sorrowes*, many forrowes take;
And I fhould moane but for one mifery,
Where now for thoufands, my poore heart doth ake.
Bide from me *Ioy* then, that oft from me bid'ft,
Be prefent *Care*, that often prefent art;
Hide from me *Comfort*, that at all times hid'ft,
For I will greeue; with a true-greeuing heart.
Ile glut my felfe with forrow for the nonce,
What though my Reafon would the fame gaine-fay?
Oh beare with my vnbridled Paffion once,
I hope it fhall not much from vertue ftray,
   Sith griefe for fuch a loffe, at fuch a feafon,
   Paft meafure may be, but not out of Reafon.

Eleg. 3.

What need I for th'infernall *Furies* hallo?
Call vpon darkneffe, and the lonely night?
Or fummon vp *Minerua*, or *Apollo*,
To helpe me dolefull Elegies endite?
Heere wants no mention of the feares of *Stix*,
Of blacke *Cocitus*, or fuch fained ftuffe:
Thofe may paint out their griefes with forced tricks,
That haue not in them reall caufe enough;
I need it not; yet for no priuate Croffe,
Droopes my fad foule, nor doe I mourne for fafhion,
For why? a generall, a publique loffe,
In me hath kindled a right wofull Paffion.
   Then (oh alas) what need hath he to borrow,
   That's pinch't already with a feeling forrow?

Firft

Prince Henries *Obsequies.*

Eleg. 4.

First, for thy losse, poore world-diuided Ile,
My eyes pay griefes drink-offering of teares :
And I set-by all other thoughts a while,
To feede my minde the better on my cares.
I saw, how happy thou wert but of late
In thy sweet *Henries* hopes, yea I saw too,
How thou didst glory in thy blessed state :
Which thou indeed hadst cause enough to doe.
But, when I saw thee place all thy delight
Vpon his worth ; and then, when thou didst place it,
*(*And thy *Ioy* almost mounted to her height)
His haplesse end so suddainely deface it ;
   Me thought, I felt it goe so neere my heart,
   Mine ak't to, with a sympathizing smart.

Eleg. 5.

For thee great *Iames*, my springs of sorrow runne,
For thee my *Muse* a heauy song doth sing ;
That hast lost more in losing of thy Sonne,
Then they that lose the title of a King.
Needs must the paines that doe disturbe the head
Difease the body throughout euery part ;
I therefore, should haue seem'd a member dead,
If I had had no feeling of this smart ;
But oh I grieue : and yet I grieue the lesse,
Thy Kingly gift so well preuail'd to make him
Fit for a Crowne of endlesse happinesse ;
And that it was th'Almighties hand, did take him,
   Who was himselfe, a booke for Kings to pore on :
   And might haue bin thy ΒΑΣΙΛΙΚΟΝ ΔΩΡΟΝ.

For

Prince Henries *Obsequies*.

Eleg. 6.

For our faire Queene, my griefe is no leffe mouing,
There's none could ere more iuftly boaft of childe:
For he was euery way moft nobly louing,
Moft full of manfull courage, and yet milde.
Me thinks I fee what heauy difcontent
Be-clouds her brow, and ouer-fhades her eyne:
Yea, I doe feele her louing heart lament,
An earneft thought conueyes the griefe to mine.
I fee fhe notes the fadneffe of the Court,
Thinks how that heere, or there fhe faw him laft:
Remembers his fweet fpeech, his gracefull fport,
And fuch like things to make her Paffion laft.
    But what meane I? Let griefe my fpeeches fmother,
    No tongue can tell the forrowes of the Mother.

Eleg. 7.

Nor thine fweet *Charles*, nor thine *Elizabeth*,
Though one of you haue gain'd a Princedome by't:
The griefe he hath to haue it by the death
Of his fole brother, makes his heart deny't,
Yet let not Sorrowes blacke obfcuring clowd
Quite couer and eclipfe all comforts light:
Though one faire Star aboue our height doth fhrowd,
Let not the Earth be left in darknes quite.
Thou *Charles* art now our Hope, God grant it be
More certaine than our laft; wee truft it will:
Yet we fhall haue a louing feare of thee;
The burned childe the fire much dreadeth ftill.
    But God loues his; and what ere forrowes threat,
    I, one day, hope to fee him *Charles* the Great.

                              Then

Prince Henries *Obsequies.*
Eleg. 8.
Then droop not *Charles* to make our griefes the more ;
God that to scourge vs, tooke away thy brother.
To comfort vs againe, kept thee in store :
And now I thinke on't *Fate* could doe no other.
Thy Father both a Sunne, and *Phœnix* is,
Prince *Henry* was a Sunne and *Phœnix* too,
And if his Orbe had beene as high as his,
His beames had shone as bright's his fathers doo.
Nature saw this and tooke him quite away,
And now dost thou to be a *Phœnix* trie ;
Well, so thou shalt (no doubt) another day,
But then thy father (*Charles*) or thou must die.
 For 'twas decreed when first the world begun,
 Earth should haue but one *Phœnix*, heau'n one Sun.
Eleg. 9.
But shall I not be-moane the sad *Elector* ?
Yes *Fredericke*, I needs must grieue for thee :
Thou wooest with woe now, but our best protector
Giues ioyfull ends where hard beginnings be.
Had we no showes to welcome thee to Court,
No solemne sight but a sad Funerall ?
Is all our former Masking and our sport,
Transform'd to sighes ? are all things tragicall ?
Had'st thou beene here at Summer, or at Spring,
Thou shouldst not then haue seene vs drooping thus,
But now tis *Autumne*, that spoiles eu'ry thing :
Vulgarly term'd the *Fall oth' leafe*, with vs.
 And not amisse ; for well may't be the Fall,
 That brings down blossoms, Fruit, leaues, tree & all,
           Then,

Prince Henries *Obsequies.*

Eleg. 10.

Then, Stranger Prince, if thou neglected seeme,
And hast not entertainement to thy State:
Our loues yet doe not therefore mis-esteeme;
But lay the fault vpon vnhappy Fate.
Thou found'st vs glad of thy arriuall here,
And saw'st him, whom we lou'd (poore wretched Elues;)
Say: didst thou ere of one more worthy heare?
No, no, and therefore now we hate our selues.
We being then of such a gem bereft,
Beare with our passions; and since one is gone,
And thou must haue the halfe of what is left;
Oh thinke on vs for good, when you are gone,
    And as thou now dost beare one halfe of's name;
    Helpe beare our griefe, and share thou all his fame.

Eleg. 11.

See, see, faire Princesse, I but nam'd thee yet,
Meaning thy woes within my breast to smother:
But on my thoughts they doe so liuely beat,
As if I heard thee sighing, *Oh my Brother:*
Me thinkes I heard thee calling on his name,
With plaining on his too-vngentle Fate:
And sure, the *Sisters* were well worthie blame,
To shew such spite to one that none did hate.
I know thou sometime musest on his face,
(Faire as a womans; but more manly-faire;)
Sometime vpon his shape, his speech, and pase,
A thousand waies thy griefes themselues repaire.
    And oh! no maruell, since your sure-pure loues
    Were neerer, dearer, than the Turtle Doues.

    How

Prince Henries *Obsequies.*

Eleg. 12.

How often, oh how often did he vow
To grace thy ioyfull lookt-for Nuptialls:
But oh how wofull, oh how wofull now
Will they be made through thefe fad Funeralls!
All pleafing parlies that betwixt you two,
Publicke, or priuate, haue exchanged beene,
All thou haft heard him promife for to doe,
Or by him in his life performed feene,
Calls on remembrance: the fweet name of Sifter
So oft pronounc't by him feemes to take place,
Of *Queene* and *Empreffe*, now my thoughts do whifper,
Thofe titles one day fhall thy vertues grace.
   If I fpeake true, for his fweet fake that's dead,
   Seeke how to raife deiected *Britaines* head.

Eleg. 13.

Seeke how to raife deiected *Britaines* head,
So fhe fhall ftudy how to raife vp thine,
And now leaue off thy teares in vaine to fhed,
For why? to fpare them I haue powr'd out mine.
Pittie thy felfe, and vs, and mournefull *Rhine*,
That hides his faire banke vnder flouds of griefe,
Thy Prince, thy Duke, thy braue Count *Palatine:*
Tis time his forrowes fhould haue fome reliefe.
Hee's come to be another brother to thee,
And helpe thy father to another fonne:
He vowes thee all the feruice loue can doe thee;
And though acquaintance hath with griefe begunne,
   Tis but to make you haue the better taft
   Of that true bliffe you fhall enioy at laft.

                      Thy

Prince Henries Obsequies.

Eleg. 14.

Thy brother's well and would not change estates,
With any Prince that raignes beneath the Skie:
No not with all the worlds great Potentates,
His plumes haue borne him to Eternitie.
Saturne rul'd in the houre of his death. He raignes o're *Saturne* now, that raign'd o're him;
He feares no Planets dangerous aspect:
But doth aboue their constellations clime,
And earthly ioyes, and sorrowes both neglect.
We saw he had his Spring amongst vs here,
He saw his Summer, but he skipt it ouer:
And Autumne now hath tane away our deare,
The reason's this, which we may plaine discouer,
    He shall escape, (for so the Almighty wils)
    The stormy Winter of ensuing ils.

Eleg. 15.

I grieue to see the wofull face oth' Court,
And for each grieued member of the land;
I grieue for those that make these griefes their sport,
And cannot their owne euill vnderstand.
I also grieue, to see how vices swarme,
And Vertue as despis'd, grow out of date:
How they receiue most hurt, that doe least harme,
And how poore honest Truth incurreth hate.
But more, much more, I grieue that we doe misse
The ioy we lately had; and that he's gone,
Whose liuing presence might haue helpt all this:
His euerlasting Absence makes me mone,
    Yea most I grieue, that *Britaines* hope is fled,
    And that her darling, braue Prince *Henrie*'s dead.

Prince

Prince Henries *Obsequies.*
Eleg. 16.

Prince *Henrie* dead! what voyce is that we heare?
Am I awake, or dreame I, tell me whether?
If this be true; if this be true, my deare,
Why doe I stay behinde thee to doe either?
Alas my Fate compels me, I must bide
To share the mischiefes of this present age,
I am ordain'd to liue till I haue tride
The very worst and vtmost of their rage:
But then why morne I not to open view,
In sable robes according to the Rites?
Why is my hat, without a branch of yeugh?
Alas my minde, no complement delights,
    Because my griefe that Ceremonie lothes,
    Had rather be in heart, than seeme in clothes.

Eleg. 17.

Thrise happy had I been, if I had kept
Within the circuit of some little Village,
In ignorance of Courts and Princes slept,
Manuring of an honest halfe-plough tillage:
Or else I would I were as young agen,
As when *Eliza* our last *Phœnix* dy'd:
My childish yeares had not conceiued then,
What 'twas to lose a Prince so dignifi'd.
But now I know: and what now doth't auaile?
Alas, whilst others merry, feele no paine,
I melancholly, sit alone and waile:
Thus sweetest profit, yeelds the bitterst gaine.
    By disobedience we did knowledge get,
    And, sorrow, euer since hath followed it,

Prince Henries *Obsequies.*

Eleg. 18.

When as the firſt ſad rumour fill'd my eare
Of *Henries* fickeneſſe ; an amazing terror
Strucke through my body, with a ſhuddring feare,
Which I expounded but my frailties error.
For though a quick-miſdoubting of the worſt,
Seem'd to fore-tell my ſoule, what would enſue :
God will forbid, thought I, that ſuch a curſt
Or ill-preſaging thought, ſhould fall out true :
It cannot ſinke into imagination,
That He, whoſe future glories we may ſee
To be at leaſt all *Europes* expectation,
Should in the prime of age deſpoiled be ;
   For if a hope ſo likely nought auaile vs,
   It is no wonder if all other faile vs.

Eleg. 19.

Againe, when one had forc't vnto my eare,
My Prince was dead; although he much proteſted,
I could not with beliefe his ſad newes heare :
But would haue ſworne, and ſworne againe, he ieſted.
At ſuch a word, me thought the towne ſhould ſinke,
The earth ſhould downe vnto the Center cleaue,
Deuouring all in her hell-gaping chinke,
And not ſo much as Sea or Iland leaue.
Some Comet, or ſome monſtrous blazing-Starre,
Should haue appear'd ; or, ſome ſtrange prodigie,
Death might haue ſhown't vs though't had bin afarre,
That he entended ſome ſuch tyranny.
   But God (it ſeemeth) did thereof diſlike,
   To ſhew that he will on a ſudden ſtrike.

Thus

Prince Henries *Obſequies*.

Eleg. 20.

Thus vnbeleeuing, I did oft enquire
Of one, of two, three, and ſo of many:
And ſtill I heard what I did leaſt deſire,
Yet grounded *Hope*, would giue no faith to any.
Then at the laſt my heart began to feare,
But as I credence to my feares was giuing
A voyce of comfort I began to heare:
Which to my fruitleſſe *Ioy* ſaid *Henrie's* liuing;
At that ſame word, my *Hope* that was forſaking
My heart, and yeelding wholly to deſpaire;
Reuiued ſtraight, and better courage taking,
Her crazed parts, ſo ſtrongly did repaire.
    I thought ſhe would haue held it out; but vaine;
    For oh, ere long, ſhe loſt it quite againe.

Eleg. 21.

But now my tongue can neuer make relation,
What I ſuſtain'd in my laſt foughten field;
My mind aſſailed with a three-fold paſſion,
Hope, Feare, Deſpaire, could vnto neither yeeld.
Feare willed me, to view the skies blacke colour,
Hope ſaid; *Vpon his hopefull vertues looke*:
Deſpaire ſhew'd me an vniuerſall dolour,
Yet fruitleſſe *Doubt*, my hearts poſſeſſion tooke:
But when I ſaw the *Hearſe*, then I beleeu'd,
And then my ſorrow was at full, alas,
Beſide, to ſhow I had not cauſeleſſe grieu'd,
I was enform'd that he embowell'd was.
    And 'twas ſubſcrib'd; they found he had no gall,
    Which I belieu'd: for he was ſweetneſſe all.

Prince Henries *Obsequies.*

Eleg. 22.

Oh cruell and infatiable *Death!*
Would none fuffice, would none fuffice but he ?
What pleafure was it more to ftop his breath,
Than to haue choakt, or kill'd, or poyfon'd me ?
My life for his, with thrice three millions more,
We would haue giuen as a ranfome to thee,
But fince thou in his loffe haft made vs poore,
Foule Tyrant, it fhall neuer honour doe thee :
For thou haft fhowne thy felfe a fpightfull fiend,
Yea Death thou didft enuy his happy ftate,
And therefore thought'ft to bring it to an end ;
But fee, fee whereto God hath turn'd thy hate.
   Thou meant'ft to marre the bliffe he had before :
   And by thy fpight, haft made it ten-times more.

Eleg. 23.

'Tis true I know, Death with an equall fpurne,
The lofty Turret, and low Cottage beats :
And takes imperially each, in his turne,
Yea though he bribes, prayes, promifes, or threats.
Nor Man, Beaft, Plant, nor Sexe, Age nor degree
Preuailes againft his dead-fure ftriking hand :
For then, ere we would thus difpoyled be,
All thefe conioyn'd his fury fhould withftand.
But oh! vnfeene he ftrikes at vnaware,
Difguifed like a murthering *Iefuite* :
Friends cannot ftop him that in prefence are ;
And which is worfe, when he hath done his fpite,
   He carries him, fo farre away from hence,
   None liues, that hath the powre to fetch him thence.

                                                Nor

Prince Henries Obsequies.

Eleg. 24.

Nor would we now, becaufe we doe beleeue
His God (to whom indeed he did belong)
To crowne him, where he hath no caufe to greeue,
Tooke him from death, that fought to doe him wrong.
But were this deare, beloued, Prince of ours
Liuing in any corner of this All,
Though kept by *Romes* and *Mahomets* chiefe powers;
They fhould not long detaine him there in thrall:
We would rake *Europe* rather, plaine the *Eaft*;
Difpeople the whole *Earth* before the Doome:
Stampe halfe to powder, and fier all the reft;
No craft, nor force, fhould him deuide vs from:
   We would breake downe what ere fhould him confine,
   Though 'twere the *Alpes*, or hilles of *Appenine*.

Eleg. 25.

But what? fhall we goe now difpute with God,
And in our hearts vpbraide him that's fo iuft?
Let's pray him rather, to withdraw his rod,
Left in his wrath he bruife vs vnto duft.
Why fhould we lay his death to Fate, or times?
I know there hath no fecond caufes bin,
But our loud crying and abhorred crimes,
Nay, I can name the chiefeft murth'ring fin:
And this it was, how-ere it hath beene hid,
Truft not (faith *Dauid*) *truft not to a Prince*;
Yet we hop't leffe, in God (I feare we did)
In iealoufie he therefore tooke him hence.
   Thus we abufe good things, and through our blindnes
   Haue hurt our felues, & kild our Prince with kindnes.

Prince Henries *Obsequies*.

Eleg. 26.

Let all the world come and bewayle our lot,
Come *Europe*, *Aſia*, *Affrica*, come all :
Mourne *Engliſh*, *Iriſh*, *Brittiſh*, and mourne *Scot*,
For his, (no I miſtake it) for our fall.
The prop of Vertue, and mankinds delight,
Hath fled the earth, and quite forſaken vs :
We had but of his excellence a ſight,
To make our longings like to *Tantalus*.
What ſeeke you in a man that he enioy'd not ?
Wert't either gift of body or of ſpirit ;
Nay, which is more, what had he, he imploy'd not
To helpe his Countrey, and her loue to merit ?
  But ſee what high preferment Vertues bring,
  He's of a ſeruant now become a King.

Eleg. 27.

But ſoft, I meane not heare to blaze his praiſe,
It is a worke too mighty, and requires
Many a Pen, and many yeeres of dayes :
My humble quill to no ſuch taske aſpires,
Onely I mourne, with deep-deep-ſighing grones,
Yet could I wiſh the other might be done ;
Though all the *Muſes* were imploy'd at once,
And write as long as *Helicon* would runne ;
But oh, I feare the Spring's already dry,
Or elſe why flags my lazie *Muſe* ſo lowe ?
Why vent I ſuch dull-ſprighted *Poeſy* ?
Surely 'tis ſunke ; I lye, it is not ſo :
  For how iſt likely that ſhould want ſupplies,
  When all we feed it with our weeping eyes ?

May

Prince Henries *Obsequies*.

Eleg. 28.

May not I liken *London* now to *Troy*,
As she was that same day she lost her *Hector*?
When proud *Achilles* spoyl'd her of her ioy
(And triumph't on her losses) being Victor?
May not I liken *Henry* to that *Greeke*,
That hauing a whole world vnto his share,
Intended other worlds to goe and seeke?
Oh no; I may not, they vnworthy are.
Say, whereto *England*, whereto then shall I
Compare that sweet departed Prince, and thee?
That noble King bewail'd by *Ieremy*,
Of thee, (great Prince,) shall the example be.
   And in our mourning we will equall them,
   Of woefull *Iuda* and *Ierusalem*.

Eleg. 29.

You that beheld it, when the mournfull traine
Past by the wall of his forsaken Parke,
Did not the very Groue seeme to complaine,
With a still murmure, and to looke more darke?
Did not those pleasant walkes (oh pleasing then
Whilst there he (healthfull) vsed to resort)
Looke like the shades of Death, neere some foule den?
And that place there, where once he kept his Court,
Did it not at his parting seeme to sinke?
And all forsake it like a Caue of sprights?
Did not the Earth beneath his Chariot shrinke,
As grieued for the losse of our delights?
   Yea his dumb Steed, that erst for none would tarry,
   Pac'd slow, as if he scarce himselfe could carry.

But

Prince Henries Obsequies.

Eleg. 30.

But oh! when it approach't th'impaled Court,
Where *Mars* himfelfe enui'd his future glory,
And whither he in armes did oft refort,
My heart conceiued a right tragicke ftory.
Whither great Prince, oh whither doft thou goe?
(Me thought the very place thus feem'd to fay)
Why in blacke roabes art thou attended fo?
Doe not (oh doe not) make fuch hafte away.
But art thou Captiue, and in triumph too?
Oh me! and worfe too, liueleffe, breathleffe, dead.
How could the Monfter-Death this mifchiefe doe?
Surely the coward tooke thee in thy bed.
    For whilft that thou art arm'd within my lift,
    He dar'd not meet thee, like a Martialift.

Eleg. 31.

Alas, who now fhall grace my turnaments:
Or honour me with deeds of Chiualry?
What fhall become of all my merriments,
My Ceremonies, fhowes of Heraldry
And other Rites? who? who fhall now adorne
Thy Sifters Nuptials with fo fweet a prefence?
Wilt thou forfake vs, leaue vs quite forlorne,
And of all ioy at once make a defeafance?
Was this the time pickt out by Deftiny?
Farewell deare Prince then, fith thou wilt be gone,
In fpight of Death goe liue eternally,
Exempt from forrow, whilft we mortals mone:
    But this ill hap inftruct me fhall to feare
    When we are ioyfull'ft, there's moft forrow neare.

                                               Then

Prince Henries *Obsequies.*

Eleg. 32.

Then, as he paſt along you might eſpye
How the grieu'd Vulgar that ſhed many a teare,
Caſt after, an vnwilling parting eye,
As loth to loſe the ſight they held ſo deare;
When they had loſt the figure of his face,
Then they beheld his roabes; his Chariot then,
Which being hid, their looke aym'd at the place,
Still longing to behold him once agen:
But when he was quite paſt, and they could finde
No obiect to employ their ſight vpon,
Sorrow became more buſie with the minde,
And drew an Armie of ſad paſſions on;
   Which made them ſo particularly mone,
   Each amongſt thouſands ſeem'd as if alone.

Eleg. 33.

And well might we of weakeſt ſubſtance melt,
With tender paſſion for his timeleſſe end,
Sith (as it ſeem'd) the purer bodies felt
Some griefe, for this their ſweet departed friend;
The Sunne wrapt vp in clowds of mournefull blacke,
Frown'd as diſpleas'd with ſuch a hainous deed,
And would haue ſtaid, or turn'd his horſes backe,
If Nature had not forte't him on with ſpeed:
Yea, and the Heauens wept a pearly dewe,
Like very teares, not ſo as if it rain'd.
His Grand-ſires tombes, as if the ſtones did rue
Our wofull loſſes; were with moyſture ſtain'd:
   Yea, either 'twas my eaſie mind's beliefe;
   Or all things were diſpoſed vnto griefe.

                                        Blacke

Prince Henries *Obsequies.*

Eleg. 34.

Blacke was *White-hall.* The windowes that did ſhine,
And double-glazed were with beauties bright,
Which Sun-like erſt did dim the gazers eyne,
As if that from within them came the light.
Thoſe to my thinking ſeemed nothing faire,
And were obſcur'd with woe, as they had been
Hung all with ſacke, or ſable-cloth of haire,
Griefe was without, and ſo 'tappear'd within.
Great was the multitude, yet quiet tho
As if they were attentiue vnto ſorrow:
The very winds did then forbeare to blow,
The Time, of flight, her ſtilneſſe ſeem' to borrow.
 Yea, all the troope pac't ſlowe, as loth to rend
 The earth that ſhould embrace their Lord & friend.

Eleg. 35.

Me thought ere-while I ſaw Prince *Henries* Armes
Aduanc't aboue the Capitoll of *Rome,*
And his keene blade, in ſpight of ſteele or charmes,
Giue many mighty enemies their doome;
Yea I had many Hopes, but now I ſee
They are ordain'd to be anothers taske:
Yet of the *Stewards* line a branch ſhall be
T' aduance beyond the *Alpes* his plumed Caske;
Then I perhaps, that now tune dolefull layes,
Amongſt their zealous triumphs may preſume
To ſing at leaſt ſome petty Captaines praiſe:
Meane-while I will ſome other worke aſſume.
 Or rather, ſith my hope-fulſt Patron's dead,
 Goe to ſome Deſert, and there hide my head.

            Had

Prince Henries Obsequies.
Eleg. 36.

Had he beene but my *Prince* and wanted all
Those ornaments of *Vertue* that so grac't him,
My loue and life had both beene at his call,
For that his *Fortune* had aboue vs plac'd him:
But his rare hopefulnesse, his flying *Fame*,
His knowledge, and his honest policie,
His courage much admir'd, his very name,
His publicke loue, and priuate curtesie:
Ioyn'd with religious firmenesse, might haue mou'd
Pale *Enuy* to haue prais'd him, and sure he,
Had he beene of meane birth; had bin belou'd;
For trust me, his sweet parts so rauish't me.
    That (if I erre, yet pardon me therefore)
    I lou'd him as my *Prince*: as *Henry* more.

Eleg: 37.

Me thought his Royall person did fore-tell
A Kingly statelines, from all pride cleare:
His looke maiesticke seemed to compell
All men to loue him, rather than to feare.
And yet though he were eu'ry good mans ioy,
And the alonely comfort of his owne,
His very name with terror did annoy
His foraine foes so farre as he was knowne.
Hell droopt for feare, the turkie *Moone* look't pale,
Spaine trembled, and the most tempestuous sea
(Where *Behemoth* the *Babylonish* Whale,
Keeps all his bloody and imperious plea)
    Was swolne with rage, for feare he'd stop the tide,
    Of her ore-daring and insulting pride.

                      For

Prince Henries *Obsequies*.

Eleg. 38.

For amongst diuers *Vertues* rare to finde,
Though many I obseru'd, I markt none more
Than in *Religion* his firme constant minde ;
Which I set deepe vpon *Remembrance* score.
And that made *Romists* for his fortunes sorry :
When therefore they shall heare of this ill hap,
Those Mints of mischiefes will extreamely glory,
That he is caught by him whom none shall scape,
Yet boast not *Babel*, thou insultst in vaine,
Thou hast not yet obtain'd the victory;
We haue a *Prince* still, and our King doth raigne,
So shall his seed, and their posterity.
 For know; God that loues his, & their good tenders,
 Will neuer leaue his faith, without defenders.

Eleg. 39.

Amidst our sacred sports that very season,
Whilst for our Country and beloued *Iames*,
Preserued from that hell-bred Powder-treason,
We rung and sung with showtes, and ioyfull flames :
Me thought vpon the sodaine I espy'd
Romes damned fiends, an anticke dance begin :
The *Furies* led it that our blesse enuy'd,
And at our rites the hel-hounds seem'd to grin.
How now thought I */* more plots */* & with that thought
Prince Henry ; dead, I plainely heard one cry :
O Lord (quoth I) now they haue that they sought,
Yet let not our gladst-day, our sadst-day die.
 God seem'd to heare, for he to ease our sorrow,
 Reuiu'd that day, to die againe the morrow.
              But

373
Prince Henries *Obsequies.*

Eleg. 40.

But *Britaine, Britaine,* tell me, tell me this,
What was the reason thy chiefe curse befell
So iuſt vpon the time of thy chiefe bliſſe?
Doſt thou not know it? heare me then, Ile tell:
Thou wert not halfe halfe-thankfull for his care
And mercy that ſo well preſerued thee;
His owne, he neuer did ſo often ſpare:
Yea he thy Lord himſelfe hath ſerued thee,
Yet *Laodicia* thou, nor hot nor cold,
Secure, and careleſſe doſt not yet repent,
Thou wilt be euer ouer-daring bold,
Till thou haſt vengeance, vpon vengeance hent.
    But (oh) ſee how *Hypocrifie* doth raigne:
    I villaine, that am worſt doe firſt complaine.

Eleg. 41.

A foule confuming Peſtilence did waſte,
And lately ſpoyld thee *England* to thy terror;
But now alas, a greater plague thou haſt,
Becauſe in time thou couldſt not ſee thy error:
Hard *Froſts* thy fields and gardens haue deflowred,
Hot *Summers* hath thy fruits Conſumption bin,
Fire many places of thee hath deuoured,
And all fore-warnings to repent thy ſin.
Yet ſtill thou didſt defer't and careleſſe ſleepe,
Which heau'n perceiuing with black clouds did frowne,
And into flouds for very anger weepe,
Yea the ſalt Sea, a part of thee did drowne.
    She drown'd a part (but oh that part was ſmall)
    Now teares more ſalt, haue ouer-whelm'd vs all.

Say

Prince Henries *Obsequies.*

Eleg. 42.

Say why was *Henries* Herſe ſo glorious?
And his ſad *Funerall* ſo full of ſtate?
Why went he to his Tombe as one victorious:
Seeming as blith as when he liu'd of late?
What needed all that *Ceremonious* ſhow?
And that dead-liuing Image which they bare?
Could not *Remembrance* make vs ſmart enough,
Vnleſſe we did afreſh renew it there?
What was it, but ſome anticke curious rite,
Onely to feed the vaine beholders eyes,
To make men in their ſorrowes more delight,
Or may we rather on it moralize?
   Yes, yes, it ſhew'd that though he wanted breath,
   Yet he ſhould ride in triumph ouer death.

Eleg. 43.

How welcome now would our deare *Henry* be,
After theſe griefes were he no more than ſtraid,
And thus deem'd dead? but fie! what *Fantaſie*
Feedes my vaine thought on? *Fate* hath that denay'd.
But ſince hee's gone, we now can call to minde,
His lateſt words, and whereto they did tend:
Yea, now our blunt capacities can finde,
They plainely did prognoſticate his end.
Beſide, we finde our *Prophecies* of old,
And would perſwade our ſelues 'twas knowne of yore
By skilfull Wizards; and by them fore-told,
But then why found we not ſo much before?
   Oh marke this euer, we ne're know our ſtate,
   Nor ſee our loſſe before it be too late.

From

Prince Henries *Obſequies*.

Eleg. 44.

From paſſion thus, to paſſion could I runne,
Till I had ouer-runne a world of words,
My *Muſe* might ſhe be heard would ne're haue done
The ſubiect, matter infinite affords,
But ther's a meane in all ; with too much greeuing
We muſt not of Gods prouidence deſpaire
Like curſed *Pagans*, or men vnbeleeuing.
Tis true, the *Hopes* that we haue loſt were faire :
But we beheld him with an outward eye,
And though he in our ſight moſt worthie ſeem'd,
Yet God ſaw more, whoſe ſecrets none can ſpye,
And findes another whom we leſſe eſteem'd :
    So *Ieſſes* eldeſt *Sonnes* had moſt renowne,
    But little *Dauid* did obtaine the Crowne.

Eleg. 45.

Let vs our truſt alone in God repoſe,
Since *Princes* faile ; and maugre *Turke* or *Pope*,
He will prouide one that ſhall quaile our foes,
We ſaw he did it, when we had leſſe hope :
Let's place our *Ioyes* in him and weepe for ſin,
Yea, let's in time amend it, and fore-ſee,
(If loſſe of earthly *Hope* hath grieuous been)
How great the loſſe of heau'ns true *Ioyes* may be :
This if we doe, God will ſtretch forth his hand,
To ſtop thoſe plagues he did intend to bring,
And poure ſuch bleſſings on this mournefull Land,
We ſhall for *I O, Halleluiah* ſing :
    And our deare *Iames*, if we herein perſeuer,
    Shall haue a *Sonne* to grace his Throne for euer.

AN EPITAPH VPON THE
moſt Hopefull and All-vertuous
Henry, Prince of *Wales*.

S*Tay* Traueiler, *and read*; *did'ſt neuer heare*
In all thy iourneyes any newes or tales
Of him whom our diuided world eſteem'd ſo deare,
And named Henrie, *the braue* Prince of Wales.

Looke here within this little place he lies,
Eu'n he that was the Vniuerſall Hope :
And almoſt made this Ile Idolatrize,
See, hee's contented with a little ſcope.

Canutus. *And as the* Dane *that on* Southampton *ſtrand,*
His Courtiers idle flatteries did chide,
(*Who tearm'd him both the God of ſea and land*)
By ſhewing he could not command the Tide ;

So this, to mocke vaine Hopes, *in him began*
Dy'd ; *and here lies, to ſhew he was a man.*

A

A Suppofed Inter-locution be-
tweene the Spirit of Prince *Henry*
and *Great Britaine*.

Br. A Wake braue *Prince*, thou doft thy Country wrong
Shake off thy flumber, thou haft flept too long,
Open thy eye-lids, and raife vp thy head,
Thy Countrey and thy Friends fuppofe thee dead.
Looke vp, looke vp, the dayes are growne more fhort,
Thy *Officers* prepare to leaue thy Court.
The ftaines of Sorrow are in euery face,
And *Charles* is call'd vpon to take thy *Place*.
Awake I fay in time, and wake the rather,
Leaft *Melancholy* hurt thy Royall *Father*.
Thy weeping *Mother* wailes and wrings her hands,
Thy *Brother* and thy *Sifter* mourning ftands;
The want of that fweet company of thine,
Inly torments the louing *Prince* of *Rhine*.
   The *Beauties* of the Court are fullied o re,
They feeme not cheerefull as they did before.
The heauy *Clergie*, in their Pulpits mourne,
And thy *Attendants* looke like men forlorne.

C c   Once

Prince Henries *Obsequies.*

Once more (I say) sweet Prince, once more, arise,
See how the teares haue drown'd my watry eyes,
All my sweet tunes and former signes of gladnes
Are turn'd to *Elegies* and Songs of sadnes.
The *Trumpet* with harsh notes the ayre doth wound
And *Dump* is all the cheerefull *Drum* can sound.
Through *Wales* a dolefull *Elegy* now rings,
And heauy Songs of sorrow each man sings :
Destressed *Ireland* to, as sad as we
Cryes loud, *Oh hone, oh hone*, for want of thee.
But more *Romes Locusts* doe begin to swarme,
And their attempts with stronger *Hopes* they arme,
For taking hold of this thy *Trans-mutation,*
They plot, againe a damned toleration.
Yea *Hell* to double this our sorrowes weight,
Is new contriuing of old *Eighty-eight.*
Come then and stand against it to defend vs,
Or else their guile, their plots, or force, will end vs.
This last-last time, sweet *Prince* I bid thee rise,
Great *Britanns* droup already : each man flies,
And if thou saue vs not from our great foes,
They quickly will effect our ouer-throwes.
Oh yet he moues not vp his liuing head,
And now I feare indeed he's dead.   *Spi.* He's dead.
Brit. What voyce was that, which from the valted roofe,
Of my last words did make so plaine a proofe ?
What was it seem'd to speake aboue me so,
And sayes *he's dead?* wast *Eccho*, yea or no ? *Spi.* No.
Brit. What is it some dispos'd to flout my mone ?
Appeare : Hast thou a body, or hast none ? *Spi.* none.
                                                                Brit.

Prince Henries *Obsequies*.

Brit. Sure some illusion, oh what art? come hither
My *Princes* Ghost, or fiend, or neither.   *Spi.* Neither.
Brit. Indeed his Ghost in heauen rests I know,
Art thou some *Angel* for him, is it so?   *Spi.* So.
Brit. Doe not my Reall griefes with visions feed,
In earnest speake, art so indeed?   *Spi.* Indeed.
Brit. What power sent thee now into my Coast,
Was it my *Darling Henrie's Ghost*?   *Spi.* 's Ghost.
Brit. Th'art welcome then, thy presence gratefull is:
But tell me liues he happily in blisse: *Spi.* y's.
Brit. If so much of thee may be vnderstood,
Is the intent of this thy comming good?   *Spi.* Good.
Brit. Say, hath he there the *Fame* that here he had,
Or doth the place vnto his glory adde?   *Spi.* Adde.
Brit. May I demand what thy good errants be?
To whom is that he told to thee?   *Sp.* To thee.
Brit. Oh doth he minde me yet, sweet Spirit say,
What is thy message? Ile obey: *Spi. Obey*.
Brit. I will not to my power one tittle misse,
Doe but command, and say, doe this: *Spi.* Doe this.
Brit. But stay, it seemes that thou hast made thy choyse,
To speake with *Eccho's* most vnperfect voyce:
In plainer wise declare why thou art sent,
That I may heare with more content: *Spi.* Content.

The Spirit leaues his Eccho and ſpeakes on.

Spi. THen here me *Britaine,* heare me and beleeue
Thy *Henries* there now where he cannot grieue.
He is not ſubiect to the flye inuaſion
Of any humane, or corrupted *Paſſion.*
For then ; (although he ſorrow now forbeares)
He would haue wept himſelfe, to ſee thy teares.
But he (as good *Saints* are) of ioyes partaker,
Is iealous of the glory of his Maker :
And though the *Saints* of *Rome* may take it to them,
(Much helpe to their damnation it will doe them)
He will not on his *Maſters* right preſume,
Nor his ſmal'ſt due vnto himſelfe aſſume.
And therefore *Britaine* in the name of God,
And on the paine of his reuengefull rod ;
He here coniures thee in thy tribulation,
To make to God alone thy inuocation :
Who tooke him from thee, that but late was liuing,
For too much truſt, vnto his weakenes giuing,
Yet call'ſt thou on thy *Prince* ſtill ; as if he,
Could either *Sauiour* or *Redeemer* be :
Thou

Prince Henries *Obsequies.*

Thou tell'ſt him of the wicked *Whore* of *Rome*,
As if that he were Iudge to giue her doome.
But thou might'ſt ſee, were not thy ſight ſo dim,
Thou mak'ſt meane-while another *Whore* of him.
For what iſt for a Creatures ayde to cry,
But ſpirits whoredome ? (that's Idolatry.)
Their moſt vnpleaſing breaths that ſo invoke,
The paſſage of th'Almighties mercies choke :
And therefore if thy ſorrowes ſhall haue end,
To God thou muſt thy whole deuotions bend.
Then will thy *King* that he leaue off to mone,
God hath tane *His*, yet left him more than one.
And that he hath not ſo ſeuerely done,
As when he crau'd the *Hebrewes* onely ſonne ;
Becauſe, beſide this little bleſſed ſtore,
There's yet a poſſibility of more.
Goe tell the *Queene* his mother that's lamenting,
There is no cauſe of that her diſcontenting.
And ſay there is another in his place,
Shall doe his louing Siſters nuptials grace.
Enforme the *Palatine*, his *Nimph* of *Thame*
Shall giue his glorious *Rhine* a trebble Fame :
But vnto *Charles*, to whom he leaues his place,
Let this related be in any caſe.
Tell him he may a full poſſeſſion take
Of what his Brother did ſo late forſake ;
But bid him looke what to his place is due,
And euery Vice in generall eſchue :
Let him conſider why he was his Brother,
And plac't aboue ſo many thouſand other.

Prince Henries *Obsequies.*

Great honours haue great burthens if y'are high,
The ſtricter's your account, and the more nigh:
Let him ſhunne flatterers at any hand,
And euer firmely in Religion ſtand,
Gird on his ſword ; call for th'Almighties might,
Keepe a good conſcience, fight the *Lambes* great fight:
For when his Father ſhall ſurrender make,
The *Faiths* protection he muſt vndertake.
Then *Charles* take heed, for thou ſhalt heare a-far,
Some cry, peace, peace, that haue their hearts on war.
Let Policie Religion obey,
But let not Policie Religion ſway:
Shut from thy counſels ſuch as haue profeſt
The worſhip of that *Antichriſtian* beaſt.
For howſoe're they dawb'd with colours trim,
Their hands doe beare his marke, their heart's on him,
And though they ſeeme to ſeeke the Commons *Weale,*
'Tis but the Monſters deadly wound to heale.
Baniſh all *Romiſh* Statiſts, doe not ſup
Of that pyde-painted Drabs infectious Cup,
Yea vſe thy vtmoſt ſtrength, and all thy power
To ſcatter them that would build *Babels* tower.
Thou muſt ſometime be iudge of equity ;
And oft ſuruey e'ne thine owne family :
That at thy Table none partaker be,
That will not at *Chriſt*'s boord partake with thee :
The Lords great day is neer ; tis neer at hand,
Vnto thy combat ſee thou brauely ſtand.
For him that ouercomes, *Chriſt* keeps a Crowne,
And the great'ſt conqueſt hath the great'ſt renowne.

Be

Prince Henries *Obsequies*.

Be mercifull, and yet in mercy iuſt :
Chaſe from thy Court both wantonneſſe and luſt.
Diſguiſed faſhions from the Land caſheare,
Women, may women, and men, men appeare.
The wide-wide mouth of the blaſphemer teares
His paſſage vnto God, through all the Spheares,
Prouoking him, to turne his peacefull word
Into a bloudy double-edged ſword :
But cut his tongue, the clapper of damnation,
He may fright others with his *Vlulation*.
The Drunkard, and Adulterer, from whence
Proceeds the cauſe of dearth and peſtilence,
Puniſh with loſſe of ſubſtance, and of limbe,
He rather maimed vnto Heauen may climbe
Then tumble whole to Hell, and by his ſin,
Endanger the whole ſtate he liueth in.
Downe, downe, with Pride, and ouerthrowe Ambition ;
Grace true Deuotion, root out ſuperſtition,
Loue them that loue the Truth, and Vertue graces,
Let Honeſty, not Wealth, obtaine great places,
Begin but ſuch a courſe, and ſo perſeuer,
Thou ſhalt haue loue here, and true bliſſe for euer :
Thus much for thy new *Prince* ; now this to thee,
Britaine ; It ſhall thy charge and duty be,
To tell him now what thou haſt heard me ſay,
And when ſoeuer he commands, obey :
So if thou wilt in mind this counſell beare ;
Vnto thy ſtate haue due regard and care,
And without ſtay vnto amendment hie,
Thou ſhalt be deare to thoſe, to whom I flie.

Prince Henries Obsequies.

Brit. Oh ſtay, and doe not leaue me yet alone.
Spi. My errand's at an end, I muſt be gone.
Brit. Goe then, but let me aske one word before.
Spi. My ſpeech now failes, I may diſcourſe no more.
Brit. Yet let me craue thus much, if ſo I may,
By *Eccho* thou reply to what I ſay.   *Spi.* Say.
Brit. Firſt tell me, for his ſake thou count'ſt moſt deare,
Is *Babels* fall and *Iacobs* riſing neare?   *Spi.* Neare.
Brit. Canſt thou declare what day that worke ſhall end,
Or rather muſt we yet attend?   *Spi.* Attend.
Brit. Some Land muſt yeeld a Prince that blow to ſtrike,
May I be that ſame Land, or no, iſt like?   *Spi.* Like.
Brit. Then therefore 'tis that *Rome* beares vs ſuch ſpight:
Is ſhe not plotting now to wrong our right?   *Spi.* right.
Brit. But from her miſchiefes and her hands impure,
Canſt thou our ſafe deliuerance aſſure?   *Spi.* Sure.
Brit. Then notwithſtanding this late loſſe befell,
And we fear'd much, I truſt 'tis well.   *Spi.* 'Tis well.
Brit. Then flie thou to thy place, if this be true,
Thou God be pras'd, and Griefes adue.   *Spi.* Adue.

A

A Sonnet of Death, compoſed in Latine Rimes, and Paraphraſtically tranſlated into the ſame kinde of verſe; both, by the former Author.

*HEûs, heûs, Mors percutit, & importuné,
Quam nunquam præterit vllus impuné.
Abite Medici, non eſt ſanabile
Hoc vulnus Θανάτοῦ; ſed incurabile.*

Hark, hark, Death knocks vs vp, with importunitie,
There's none ſhall euer make boaſt of impunitie.
The Doctor toyles in vaine, mans life's not durable,
No med'cine can preuaile, this wound's incurable.

*Quid picti Dominûm proſunt fauores?
Ficti quid Hominum iuuant amores?
Nec mundi vanitas, nec Pompa Curiæ,
Poteſt reſiſtere Mortis iniuriæ.*

What will the countenance of Lords, or Noble-men
Or idle peoples loue, helpe or auaile thee then?
Nor the worlds brauery, nor yet Court vanitie,
Can ſtay this Monſters hand, foe to humanitie.

*Non curat ſplendidum, nec Venerabile;
Nec pectus candidum quamuis amabile;*

Decumbunt

Prince Henries Obsequies.

Decumbunt Principes iniquo vulnere.
Heu parcit nemini, quin strauit puluere.

He knowes no reuerence, nor cares for any state,
Sweet beauties moue him not, though nere so delicate,
Princes must stoope to him, he rides on martially,
And spares not any man, but strikes impartially.

Mercede diuitis nil morat cupidi,
Nec prece pauperis (si orat) miseri,
Et frustra fallere tentas ingenio,
Surda Rhetorici Mors est eloquio.

The rich-mans money-bags are no perswasion,
The beggers wofull cry, stirres vp no passion,
Hee'l not beguiled be, by any fallacy,
Nor yeeld to Rhetoricke, Wit, Art, nor Policy.

Aspectu pallida, vultu terribilis ;
Est tamen valida, Mors iunincibilis :
Et suas tibias (nec est formalis)
Vir omnis sequitur, si sit mortalis.

His look's both pale and wan, yet doth it terrifie,
He masters any man (alas what remedy !)
He's nothing curious which way the measures be,
But all dance after him, that heare his melodie.

At oh ! oh horrida, lætans necando,
Ruit incognita ; non scimus quando :

Et

Prince Henries *Obsequies*.

Et statim perditur hæc mundi gloria:
Vita sic fragilis, sic transitoria.

But wo! of all the rest this seemes most terrible,
He comes when we know least, and then inuisible,
Then quite there endeth all worldly prosperitie,
Such is this lifes estate, such his seueritie.

Ergo vos incolæ terrarum timidi,
Este soliciti, vos, oh vos miseri!
Sic (quamuis subita;) hæc è carnalibus,
Reddet vos similes, dijs immortalibus.

Then oh you wretched men, sith this is euident,
See you more carefull be, oh be more prouident,
And when he takes this life, full of incertaintie;
You shall liue euer-more, to all eternitie.

FINIS.

A
SATYRE,
Written to the *KINGS*
moſt Excellent Maieſtie,

BY

GEORGE WITHER,

When hee was Priſoner in the
Marſhallſey, for his firſt
BOOKE.

LONDON:
Printed by *T. S.* for *Iohn Budge*, dwelling in *Pauls-*
Church-yard, at the ſigne of the Greene
Dragon, 1622.

The Satyre to the
meere Courtiers.

Irs; *I doe know your mindes; You looke for
    fees,*
*For more respect then needes, for caps and
    knees.*
But be content, I haue not for you now ;
Nor will I haue at all to doe with you.
For, though I seeme opprest, and you suppose
I must be faine to crouch to Vertues foes ;
Yet know, your fauours I doe sleight them more
In this distresse, then ere I did before.
Here

A Satyre.

Here to my Liege *a message I must tell;*
If you will let me passe, you shall doe well;
If you denie admittance, why then know,
I meane to haue it where you will or no.
Your formall wisedome which hath neuer beene
In ought but in some fond inuention seene,
And you that thinke men borne to no intent,
But to be train'd in Apish complement;
Doth now (perhaps) suppose mee indiscreet,
And such vnused messages vnmeet.
But what of that? Shall I goe sute my matter
Vnto your wits, that haue but wit to flatter?
Shall I, of your opinions so much prize
To lose my will that you may thinke me wise,
Who neuer yet to any liking had,
Vnlesse he were a Knaue, *a* Foole, *or* mad?
You Mushroms *know, so much I weigh your powers,*
I neither value you, *nor what is yours.*
Nay, though my crosses had me quite out-worne,
Spirit enough I'de finde your spight to scorne:
Of which resolu'd, to further my aduenture,
Vnto my King, *without your leaues I enter.*

To

To the Honeſt

Courtiers.

Vt You, *whoſe onely worth doth colour giue.*
To Them, *that they doe worthy ſeeme to liue,*
Kinde Gentlemen, *your ayde I craue, to bring*
A Satyre *to the preſence of his King:*
A ſhow of rudeneſſe doth my fore-head arme,
Yet you may truſt him; he intends no harme.
He that hath ſent him, loyall is, and true,
And one, whoſe loue (I know) is much to you:
But now, he lyes bound to a narrow ſcope;
Almoſt beyond the Cape of all good Hope.
Long hath he ſought to free himſelfe, but failes:
And therefore ſeeing nothing elſe preuailes,

A   Me,

Me, *to acquaint his* Soueraigne, *here he sends*,
As one despairing of all other friends.
I doe presume that you will fauour shew him,
Now that a Messenger from thence you know him.
For many thousands that his face ne're knew,
Blame his Accusers, and his Fortune *rue:*
And by the helpe which your good word may doe,
He hopes for pitty from his Soueraigne *to.*
Then in his *presence with your fauours grace him,*
And there's no Vice *so great, shall dare out-face him.*

To

To the Kings moſt Excellent
MAIESTIE.

A SATYRE.

Quid tu, ſi perco?

Hat once the *Poet* ſaid, I may auow,
'Tis a hard thing not to write Satyrs, now.
Since, what we ſpeake (abuſe raigns ſo in all)
Spight of our hearts, will be *Satyricall*.
Let it not therefore now be deemed ſtrange,
My vnſmooth'd lines their rudeneſſe do not change;
Nor be diſtaſtefull to my gracious *King*,
That in the *Cage*, my old harſh notes I ſing:
And rudely, make a *Satyre* here vnfold,
What others would in neater tearmes haue told.
And why? my friends and meanes in *Court* are ſcant,
Knowledge of curious phraſe, and forme I want.
I cannot bear't to runne my ſelfe in debt,
To hire the *Groome*, to bid the *Page* entreat,
Some *fauourd Follower* to vouchſafe his word
To get me a cold comfort from his *Lord*.
I cannot footh, (though it my life might ſaue,)
Each *Fauourite*, nor crouch to eu'ry *Knaue*.
I cannot brooke delayes as ſome men do,
With ſcoffes, and ſcornes, and tak't in kindneſſe to.
For ere I'de binde my ſelfe for ſome ſlight grace,
To one that hath no more worth then his *place*.

Dd 2   Or

A Satyre.

Or, by a *bafe meane* free my felfe from trouble,
I rather would endure my penance double:
Caufe to be forc'd to what my mind difdaines,
Is worfe to me then *tortures, rackes,* and *chaines.*
And therefore vnto *thee* I onely flye,
To whom there needs no meane but *Honefty.*
To *thee,* that lou'ft nor *Parafite* or *Minion,*
Should ere I fpeake poffeffe thee with opinion.
To *thee,* that do'ft what thou wilt vndertake,
For loue of *Iuftice,* not the *perfons* fake.
To *thee,* that know'ft how vaine all faire fhewes be,
That flow not from the hearts finceritie;
And canft, though fhadowed in the fimpleft vaile,
Difcerne both *Loue* and *Truth,* and where they faile.
To *thee* doe I appeale; in whom Heau'n knowes,
I next to God my confidence repofe.
For, can it be thy Grace fhould euer fhine,
And not enlighten fuch a Caufe as mine?
Can my hopes (fixt in thee great *King)* be dead;
Or thou thofe *Satyrs* hate thy *Forrefts* bred?
Where fhall my fecond hopes be founded then,
If euer I haue heart to hope agen?
Can I fuppofe a fauour may be got
In any place, when thy *Court* yeelds it not?
Or that I may obtaine it in the land,
When I fhall be deni'd it at thy hand?
And if I might, could I delighted be,
To tak't of others, when I mift of thee?

                                                Or

A Satyre.

Or if I were, could I haue comfort by it,
When I should thinke my *Soueraigne* did deny it?
No; were I sure, I to thy hate were borne,
To seeke for others fauours, I would scorne.
For, if the best-worth-loues I could not gaine,
To labour for the rest I would disdaine.
   But why should I thy fauour here distrust,
That haue a *cause* so knowne, and knowne so iust?
Which not alone my inward comfort doubles,
But all suppose me wrong'd that heare my troubles.
Nay, though my fault were Reall, I beleeue
Thou art so Royall, that thou wouldst forgiue.
   For, well I know, thy sacred *Maiesty*
Hath euer beene admir'd for Clemency,
And at thy gentlenesse the world hath wondred,
For making Sun-shine, where thou mightst haue thun-
Yea, thou in mercy, life to them didst giue   (dred.
That could not be content to see *thee* liue.
And can I thinke that thou wilt make me, then,
The most vnhappy of all other men?
Or let thy loyall Subiect, against reason,
Be punisht more for *Loue*, then some for *Treason*?
No, thou didst neuer yet thy glory staine
With an iniustice to the meanest *Swaine*.
'Tis not thy will I'me wrong'd, nor dost thou know,
If I haue suffred iniuries or no.
For if I haue not heard false *Rumours* flie,
Th'ast grac'st me with the stile of *Honesty*,

                                                And

A Satyre.

And if it were fo (as fome thinke it was)
I cannot fee how it fhould come to paffe
That *thou*, from whofe free *tongue* proceedeth nought
Which is not correfpondent with thy thought.
Thofe thoughts to, being fram'd in *Reafons* mould,
Should fpeake that once, which fhould not euer hold.
   But paffing it as an vncertainety,
I humbly begge thee, by that *Maiefty*,
Whofe facred *Glory* ftrikes a louing-feare
Into the hearts of all, to whom 'tis deare :
To deigne me fo much fauour, without merit,
As read this plaint of a diftempered fpirit :
And thinke, vnleffe I faw fome hideous ftorme,
Too great to be endur'd by fuch a *worme*,
I had not thus prefum'd vnto a *King*,
With *Æfops Fly*, to feeke an *Eagles* wing :
   Know I am he, that entred once the lift,
Gainft all the world to play the *Satyrift* :
Twas I, that made my meafures rough and rude,
Dance arm'd with whips amidft the multitude,
And vnappalled with my charmed *Scrowles*,
Teaz'd angry *Monfters* in their lurking holes.
I'ue plaid with *Wafpes* and *Hornets* without feares,
Till mad they grew, and fwarm'd about my eares.
I'ue done it, and me thinkes tis fuch braue fport,
I may be ftung ; but nere be forry for't.
For, all my griefe is, that I was fo fparing,
And had no more in't, worth the name of daring.
                                            Hee

A Satyre.

He that will taxe thefe times muft be more bitter,
Tart lines of *Vinegar* and *Gall* are fitter.
My fingers and my fpirits were benum'd,
My *inck* ran forth too fmooth, twas two much gum'd ;
I'de haue my *Pen* fo paint it, where it traces,
Each accent, fhould draw blood into their faces.
And make them, when their *Villanies* are blazed,
Shudder and *ftartle*, as men halfe amazed,
For feare my *Verfe* fhould make fo loud a din,
Heauen hearing might raine vengeance on their fin.
Oh now, for fuch a ftraine! would *Art* could teach it.
Though halfe my fpirits I confum'd to reach it.
Ide learne my *Mufe* fo braue a courfe to flie,
Men fhould admire the power of *Poefie*.
And thofe that dar'd her greatneffe to refift,
Quake euen at naming of a *Satyrift*.
But when his fcourging numbers flow'd with wonder,
Should cry, *God bleffe vs*, as they did at thunder.
 Alas! my lines came from me too-too dully,
They did not fill a *Satyrs* mouth vp fully.
Hot blood, and youth, enrag'd with paffions ftore,
Taught me to reach a *ftraine* nere touch'd before.
But it was coldly done, I throughly chid not:
And fomewhat there is yet to doe, I did not.
More foundly could my fcourge haue yerked many,
Which I omitted not for feare of any.
For *want of action, difcontentments rage,*
Bafe *dif-refpect of Vertue (*in this age*)*

A Satyre.

With other things which were to Goodneſſe wrong,
Made me ſo feareleſſe in my careleſſe Song:
That, had not reaſon within compaſſe won me,
I had told *Truth* enough to haue vndone me.
(Nay, haue already, if that her Diuine
And vnſeene power, can doe no more then mine.)
For though fore-ſeeing warineſſe was good,
I fram'd my ſtile vnto a milder mood;
And clogging her high-towring wings with mire,
Made her halfe earth, that was before all fire.
Though (as you ſaw) in a diſguiſed ſhew
I brought my *Satyres* to the open view:
Hoping (their out-ſides, being miſ-eſteem'd)
They might haue paſſed, but for what they ſeem'd:
Yet *ſome* whoſe *Comments* iumpe not with my minde,
In that low phraſe, a higher reach would finde,
And out of their deepe iudgements ſeeme to know,
What 'tis vncertaine if I meant or no:
Ayming thereby, out of ſome priuate hate,
To worke my ſhame, or ouer-throw my ſtate.
For, amongſt many wrongs my *foe* doth doe me,
And diuers imputations laide vnto me,
(Deceiued in his ayme) he doth miſ-conſter
That which I haue enſtil'd a *Man-like Monſter*,
To meane ſome priuate perſon in the State,
Whoſe worth I ſought to wrong out of my hate;
Vpbraiding *me*, I from my word doe ſtart,
Either for want of better *Ground*, or *Heart*.

Cauſe

A Satyre.

Caufe from his expectation I did vary
In the denying of his *Commentary,*
Whereas tis knowne I meant *Abufe* the while,
Not thinking any *one* could be fo vile
To merit all thofe *Epithites* of fhame,
How euer many doe deferue much blame.
   But fay, (I grant) that I had an intent
To haue it fo (as he interprets) meant,
And let my gracious *Liege* fuppofe there were
One whom the *State* may haue iuft caufe to feare;
Or thinke there were a man (and great in *Court*)
That had more faults then I could well report;
Suppofe I knew him, and had gone about
By fome particular markes to paint him out,
That *he* beft knowing his owne faults, might fee,
He was the *Man* I would fhould noted be:
Imagine now fuch doings in this *Age*,
And that *this man* fo pointed at, fhould rage,
Call me in queftion, and by his much threatning,
By long imprifonment, and ill-intreating
Vrge a *Confeffion*, wert not a mad part
For me to tell *him*, what lay in my heart?
Doe not I know a great mans *Power* and *Might*;
In fpight of *Innocence*, can fmother *Right*,
Colour his *Villanies*, to get efteeme,
And make the *honeft man* the *Villaine* feeme?
And that the truth I told fhould in conclufion,
For want of *Power* and *Friends* be my confufion?
                                      I know

A Satyre.

I know it, and the world doth know tis true,
Yet, I proteſt, if ſuch a man I knew,
That might my *Country* preiudice, or *Thee*,
Were he the greateſt or the proudeſt *Hee*
That breathes this day : (if ſo it might be found,
That any good to *either* might redound.)
So far Ile be (though *Fate* againſt me run)
From ſtarting off from that I haue begun,
I vn-appalled dare in ſuch a caſe
Rip vp his fouleſt *Crimes* before his face,
Though for my *labour* I were ſure to drop
Into the mouth of *Ruine* without hope.
    But ſuch ſtrange farre-fetcht meanings they haue
As I was neuer priuie to in thought ;   (ſought,
And that vnto particulars would tie
Which I intended vniuerſally.
Whereat *ſome* with diſpleaſure ouer-gone,
(Thoſe I ſcarce dream'd of, ſaw, or thought vpon)
Maugre thoſe caueats on my *Satyrs* brow,
Their honeſt and iuſt paſſage diſallow.
And on their heads ſo many cenſures rake,
That ſpight of *me*, themſelues they'le guilty make.
    Nor is't enough, to ſwage their diſcontent,
To ſay *I am* (or to be) *innocent*.
For as, when once the *Lyon* made decree,
No *horned beaſt* ſhould nigh his preſence be,
That, on whoſe fore-head onely did appeare
A *bunch of fleſh*, or but ſome *tuft of haire*,
                                 Was

A Satyre.

Was euen as farre in danger as the reſt,
If he but ſaid, it was a *horned beaſt:*
So, there be now, who thinke in that their power
Is of much force, or greater farre then our;
It is enough to proue a guilt in me,
Becauſe (miſtaking) they ſo think't to be.
   Yet 'tis my comfort, they are not ſo high,
But they muſt ſtoope to *Thee* and *Equitie.*
And this I know, though prickt; they ſtorme agen,
The world doth deeme them ne're the better men.
To ſtirre in filth, makes not the ſtench the leſſe,
Nor doth Truth *feare the frowne of* Mightineſſe.
Becauſe thoſe numbers ſhe doth daigne to grace,
Men may ſuppreſſe a while, but ne're deface.
   I wonder, and 'tis wondred at by many,
My harmeleſſe lines ſhould breed diſtaſte in any:
And ſo, that (whereas moſt *good men* approue
My labour to be worthy thankes, and loue*)*
I as a *Villaine,* and my *Countries foe,*
Should be impriſon'd, and ſo ſtrictly to,
That not alone my liberty is barr'd,
But the reſort of friends *(*which is more hard.*)*
And whilſt each wanton, or looſe *Rimers* Pen,
With oyly words, ſleekes o're the ſinnes of men,
Vayling his wits to euery *Puppets* becke,
Which ere I'le doe, I'le ioy to breake my necke.
*(*I ſay) while ſuch as they in euery place
Can finde protection, patronage and grace;

                                   If

A Satyre.

If any looke on me, 'tis but a skaunce
Or if I get a fauour, 'tis by chance.
I must protect my selfe: poore *Truth* and *I*
Can haue scarce *one* speake for our *honesty*.
Then whereas they can gold and gifts attaine,
Malitious *Hate*, and *Enuy* is my gaine,
And not alone haue here my *Freedome* lost,
Whereby my *best hope*'s likely to be crost:
But haue beene put to more charge in one day,
Then all my *Patrons* bounties yet will pay.
What I haue done, was not for thirst of *gaine*,
Or out of hope *preferments* to attaine.
Since to contemne them, would more profit me,
Then all the *glories* in the world that be:
Yet they are helpes to *Vertue*, vs'd aright,
And when they wanting be, she wants her might.
For Eagles mindes ne're fit a Rauens feather,
To dare, and to be able, sute together.
    But what is't I haue done so worthy blame,
That some so eagerly pursue my fame?
Vouchsafe to view't with thine owne eyes, and trie
(Saue want of *Art*) what fault thou canst espie.
I haue not sought to scandalize the State,
Nor sowne sedition, nor made publike hate:
I haue not aym'd at any good mans fame,
Nor taxt (directly) any one by name.
I am not he that am growne discontent
With the Religion; or the Gouernement.
                                      I meant

A Satyre.

I meant no Ceremonies to protect,
Nor doe I fauour any new-sprung Sect;
But to my Satyres *gaue this onely warrant,*
To apprehend and punish Vice *apparant.*
Who aiming in particular at none,
In generall vpbraided euery one:
That each (vnshamed of himselfe) might view
That in himselfe, which no man dares to shew.
    And hath this *Age* bred vp neat *Vice* so tenderly,
She cannot brooke it to be touch'd so slenderly?
Will she not bide my gentle *Satyres* bites?
Harme take her then, what makes she in their sights?
If with impatience she my *Whip-cord* feele,
How had she raged at my lash of *Steele*?
But am I call'd in question for her cause?
Is't *Vice* that these afflictions on me drawes?
And need I now thus to Apologize,
Onely because I scourged *Villanies*?
Must I be faine to giue a reason why,
And how I dare allow of *Honesty*?
Whilst that each fleering *Parasite* is bold
Thy Royall brow vndaunted to behold:
And euery *Temporizer* strikes a string,
That's Musicke for the hearing of a King?
Shall not *he* reach out to obtaine as much,
Who dares more for thee then a hundred such?
Heauen grant her patience, *my* Muse *takes't so badly,*
I feare shee'le lose her wits, for she raues madly.
                                                  Yet

A Satyre.

Yet let not my *dread Soueraigne* too much blame her,
Whofe awfull prefence, now hath made her tamer.
For if there be no *Fly* but hath her fpleene,
Nor a poore *Pifmire*, but will wreake her teene;
How fhall I then, that haue both fpleene and gall,
Being vniuftly dealt with, beare with all?
I yet with *patience* take what I haue borne,
And all the worlds enfuing hate can *fcorne*:
But 'twere in me as much ftupiditie,
Not to haue feeling of an iniurie,
As it were weakeneffe not to brooke it well:
What others therefore thinke I cannot tell;
But he that's leffe then *mad*, is more then *Man*,
Who fees when he hath done the beft he can,
To keepe within the bounds of *Innocence*:
Sought to difcharge his due to *God* and *Prince*.
That he, whilft *Villanies* vnreproued goe,
Scoffing, to fee him ouer-taken fo,
Should haue his *good endeauours* mifconceiu'd,
Be of his *deareft liberty* bereau'd;
And which is worfe, without reafon why,
Be frown'd on by *Authorities* grim eye.
By that great Power *my foule fo much doth feare,*
She fcornes the ftearn'ft frownes of a mortall Peere.
But that I *Vertue* loue, for her owne fake,
It were enough to make me vndertake
To fpeake as much in praife of *Vice* agen,
And practife fome to plague thefe *fhames of men*.

I meane

A Satyre.

I meane thofe my *Accufers*, who miftaking
My aymes, doe frame conceits of their owne making.
But if I lift, I need not buy fo deere
The iuft *reuenge* might be inflicted here.
Now could I *meafures* frame in this iuft fury,
Should fooner finde fome guilty then a *Iury:*
The *words*, like *fwords* (temper'd with *Art*) fhould pierce
And hang, and draw, and quarter them in verfe.
Or I could racke them on the wings of *Fame*,
(*And he's halfe hang'd* (they fay) *hath an ill name*)
Yea, I'de goe neere to make thofe guilty Elues,
Lycambes-like, be glad to hang themfelues :
And though this *Age* will not abide to heare
The faults reprou'd, that *Cuftome* hath made deare ;
Yet, if I pleafed, I could write their *crimes*,
And pile them vp in wals for after-times :
For they'le be glad (perhaps) that fhall enfue,
To fee fome ftory of their Fathers true.
Or fhould I fmother'd be in darkneffe ftill,
I might not vfe the freedome of a quill :
'Twould raife vp *brauer fpirits* then mine owne,
To make my caufe, and this their guilt more knowne.
Who by that fubiect fhould get Loue and Fame,
Vnto my foes difgrace, and endleffe fhame :
Thofe I doe meane, whofe *Comments* haue mif-us'd me :
And to thofe Peeres I honour, haue accus'd me :
Making againft *my Innocence* their batteries,
And wronging *them* by their bafe flatteries.
                                        But

A Satyre.

But of reuenge I am not yet fo faine,
To put my felfe vnto that needleffe paine:
Becaufe I know a greater *Power* there is,
That noteth fmaller iniuries then this;
And being ftill as iuft as it is ftrong,
Apportions due reuenge for euery wrong.
    But why (fome fay) fhould his too faucy Rimes
Thus taxe the wife and great ones of our times?
It fuites not with his yeeres to be fo bold,
Nor fits it vs by him to be controld.
I muft confeffe ('tis very true indeed)
Such fhould not of my cenfure ftand in need.
But blame me not, I faw good *Vertue* poore,
Defert, among the moft, thruft out of doore,
Honeftie hated, *Curtefie* banifhed,
Rich men exceffiue, *poore men* famifhed:
Coldneffe in *Zeale*, in *Lawes* partialitie,
Friendfhip but *Complement*, and vaine *Formalitie*,
Art I perceiue contem'd, while moft aduance
(To offices of worth) *Rich Ignorance*:
And thofe that fhould our *Lights* and *Teachers* be
Liue (if not worfe) as wantonly as we.
Yea, I faw *Nature* from her courfe runne backe,
Diforders grow, *Good Orders* goe to wracke.
So to encreafe what all the reft beganne,
I to this current of *confufion* ranne.
And feeing Age, left off the place of guiding,
Thus plaid the faucy wagge, and fell to chiding.
                                        Wherein

A Satyre.

Wherein, how euer fome *(*perhaps) may deeme,
I am not fo much faulty as I feeme :
For when the *Elders* wrong'd *Sufanna's* honer,
And none withftood the Shame they laid vpon her;
A *Childe* rofe vp to ftand in her defence,
And fpight of wrong confirm'd her *Innocence:*
To fhew, *thofe muft not, that good vndertake,*
Straine curt'fie, who fhall do't, for manners fake.
Nor doe I know, whether to me God gaue
A boldneffe more then many others haue,
That I might fhew the world what fhamefull blot
Vertue by her lafciuious *Elders* got.
Nor is't a wonder, as fome doe fuppofe,
My *Youth* fo much corruption can difclofe;
Since euery day the Sunne doth light mine eyes,
I am informed of new villanies :
But it is rather to be wondred how
I either can, or dare be honeft now.

And though againe there be fome others rage,
That I fhould dare (fo much aboue mine age)
Thus cenfure each degree, both young and old,
I fee not wherein I am ouer-bold.
For if I haue beene plaine with *Vice,* I care not,
There's nought that I know good, and can, and dare not.
Onely this one thing doth my minde deterre,
Euen a feare (through ignorance) to erre.

But oh knew I, what thou would'ft well approue,
Or might the fmall'ft refpect within thee moue;

A Satyre.

So in the fight of God it might be good,
And with the quiet of my confcience ftood:
(As well I know thy true integrity
Would command nothing againſt Piety:)
There's nought fo dangerous, or full of feare,
That for my *Soueraignes* fake I would not dare:
Which good beliefe, would it did not poffeffe thee;
Prouided fome iuft triall might rebleffe me:
Yea, though a while I did endure the gall
Of thy difpleafure in this loathfome thrall.
For notwithſtanding in this *place* I lye
By the command of that *Authoritie*,
Of which I haue fo much refpectiue care,
That in mine *owne* (and iuft) defence I feare
To vfe the free fpeech that I doe intend,
Leſt *Ignorance*, or *Raſhneſſe* ſhould offend.
Yet is my meaning and my thought as free
From wilfull wronging of thy *Lawes* or *Thee*,
As he to whom thy *Place* and *Perfons* deareft,
Or to himfelfe that finds his confcience cle aeft.
If there be *wrong*, 'tis not my making it,
All the offence is fome's miftaking it.
And is there any Iuſtice borne of late,
Makes thoſe faults mine, which others perpetrate?
What man could euer any Age yet finde,
That fpent his fpirits in this thankeleffe kinde,
Shewing his meaning, to fuch words could tye it,
That none could either wrong, or mif-apply it.
                                                Nay,

A Satyre.

 Nay, your owne *Lawes*, which (as you doe intend)
In plain'ſt and moſt effectuall words are penn'd,
Cannot be fram'd ſo well to your intent,
But ſome there be will erre from what you meant.
And yet (alas) I muſt be ty'de vnto
What neuer any man before could doe?
Muſt all I ſpeake, or write, ſo well be done
That none may pick more meanings thence then one?
Then all the world (I hope) will leaue diſ-vnion,
And euery man become of one opinion.
But ſince ſome may, what care ſoe're we take,
Diuers conſtructions of our Writings make,
The honeſt *Readers* euer will conceaue
The beſt intention's, and all others leaue:
Chiefly in *that*, where I fore-hand proteſt
My meaning euer was the honeſteſt,
And if I ſay ſo, what is he may know
So much as to affirme it was not ſo?
Sit other men ſo neare my thoughts to ſhow it,
Or is my *heart* ſo open that all know it?
Sure if it were, they would no ſuch things ſee,
As thoſe whereof ſome haue accuſed mee.
But I care leſſe how it be vnderſtood,
Becauſe the heauens know my intent was good.
And if it be ſo, that my too-free *Rimes*
Doe much diſpleaſe the world, and theſe bad times;
'Tis not my fault, for had I been imploy'd
In ſomething elſe, all this had now been voyd.

A Satyre.

Or if the world would but haue granted me
Wealth, or Affaires, whereon to busie me,
I now vnheard of, peraduenture than,
Had been as mute as some rich *Clergie-man*.
    But they are much deceiu'd that thinke my minde
Will ere be still, while it can doing find;
Or that vnto the world so much it leanes,
As to be curtold for default of meanes.
No, though most be, all *Spirits* are not earth,
Nor suting with the fortunes of their birth,
My *body*'s subiect vnto many Powers:
But my *soule*'s as free, as is the *Emperours*:
And though to curbe her in, I oft assay,
She'le breake int' action spite of durt and clay.
And is't not better then to take this course,
Then fall to study mischiefes and doe worse?
I say she must haue action, and she shall:
For if she will, how can I doe withall?
And let those that o're-busie thinke me, know,
He made me, that knew, why he made me so.
And though there's some that say my thoughts doe flie
A pitch beyond my states sufficiency;
My humble minde, I giue my *Sauiour* thanke
Aspires nought yet, aboue my fortunes ranke.
But say it did, wil't not befit a man
To raise his thoughts as neere *Heau'n* as he can?
Must the *free spirit* ty'd and curbed be
According to the bodies pouerty?

                                                Or

A Satyre.

Or can it euer be fo fubiect to
Bafe *Change*, to rife, and fall, as fortunes doe?
   Men borne to noble meanes, and vulgar mindes
Enioy their wealth; and there's no Law that bindes
Such to abate their fubftance, though their Pates
Want *Braines*, and they *worth*, to poffeffe fuch ftates.
So God to fome, doth onely *great mindes* giue,
And little other meanes, whereon to liue.
What law or confcience then fhall make them fmother
Their *Spirit*, which is their life, more then other
To bate their fubftance? fince if 'twere confeft,
That a braue minde could euer be fuppreft,
Were't reafon any fhould himfelfe depriue
Of what the whole world hath not power to giue?
For wealth is comon, and fooles get it to,
When to giue fpirit's more then *Kings* can do.
   I fpeake not this, becaufe I thinke there be
More then the ordinareft gifts in me;
But againft thofe, who thinke I doe prefume
On more then doth befit me to affume:
Or would haue all, whom *Fortune* barres from ftore,
Make themfelues wretched, as fhe makes them poore.
And 'caufe in other things fhe is vnkind,
Smother the matchleffe bleffings of their minde:
Whereas (although her fauours doe forfake them)
Their *minds* are richer then the world can make them.
Why fhould a good attempt difgraced feeme,
Becaufe the perfon is of meane efteeme?

              E e 3   Vertue's

A Satyre.

Vertue's *a chaste Queene*, and yet doth not scorne
To be embrac'd by him that's meanest borne,
Shee is the prop, that *Maiesties* support,
Yet one whom *Slaues* as well as *Kings* may court.
She loueth all that beare affection to her,
And yeelds to any that hath heart to wooe her.
So Vice, *how high so e're she be in place,*
Is that which Groomes *may spit at in disgrace*:
She is a strumpet, and may be abhorr'd,
Yea, spurn'd at in the bosome of a *Lord*.
Yet had I spoke her faire, I had beene free,
As many others of her Louers be.
If her escapes I had not chanc'd to tell,
I might haue beene a *villaine*, and done well:
Gotten some speciall fauour, and not sate
As now I doe, shut vp within a *grate*.
Or if I could haue hap't on some loose straine,
That might haue pleas'd the wanton Readers vaine:
Or but claw'd *Pride*, I now had been vnblam'd,
(Or else at least there's some would not haue sham'd
To plead my cause:) but see my fatall curse,
Sure I was either mad, or somewhat worse:
For I saw *Vices* followers brauely kept,
In *Silkes* they walkt, on beds of *Downe* they slept,
Richly they fed on dainties euermore,
They had their pleasure, they had all things store,
(Whil'st *Vertue* begg'd) yea, fauours had so many,
I knew they brook't not to be touch'd of any:

           Yet

A Satyre.

Yet could not I, like other men, be wife,
Nor learne *(*for all this*)* how to temporize ;
But muft (with too much honefty made blind*)*
Vpbraid this loued darling of mankind *:*
Whereas I might haue better thriu'd by fayning :
Or if I could not chufe, but be complaining,
More fafe I might haue rail'd on *Vertue* fure,
Becaufe her louers and her friends are fewer.
I might haue brought fome other things to paffe,
Made *Fidlers Songs*, or *Ballads*, like an Affe,
Or any thing almoft indeed but this.
Yet fince 'tis thus, I'me glad 'tis fo amiffe ;
Becaufe if I am guilty of a crime,
'Tis that, wherein the beft of euery time,
Hath beene found faulty (if they faulty be)
That doe reproue *Abufe* and *villany*.

    For what I'me taxt, I can examples fhow,
In fuch old *Authors* as this State allow :
And I would faine once learne a reafon why
They can haue kinder vfage here then I ?
I mufe men doe not now in queftion call
Seneca, Horace, Perfius, Iuuenall,
And fuch as they ?   Or why did not that Age
In which they liued, put them in a *Cage ?*
If I fhould fay, that men were iufter then,
I fhould neere hand be made vnfay't agen :
And therefore fure I thinke I were as good
Leaue it to others to be vnderftood.

A Satyre.

Yet I as well may fpeake, as deeme amiffe,
For fuch this *Ages* curious cunning is,
I fcarcely dare to let mine heart thinke ought,
For there be fome will feeme to know my thought,
Who may out-face me that I thinke awry,
When there's no witneffe, but my *Confcience* by :
And then I likely am as ill to fpeed,
As if I fpake, or did amiffe indeed.
  Yet left thofe who (perhaps) may malice this,
Interpret alfo thefe few lines amiffe,
Let them that after *thee*, fhall reade or heare,
From a rafh cenfure of my thoughts forbeare.
Let them not mold the fenfe that this containes
According to the forming of their braines,
Or thinke I dare, or can, here taxe thofe *Peeres*,
Whofe *Worths*, their *Honours*, to my foule endeares,
(Thofe by whofe loued-fear'd *Authority*)
I am reftrained of my liberty :
For left there yet may be a man fo ill,
To haunt my lines with his blacke *Coment* ftill,
(In hope my lucke againe may be fo good,
To haue my words once rightly vnderftood)
This I proteft, that *I doe not condemne
Ought as vniuft, that hath been done by them* ;
For though my honeft heart not guilty be
Of the leaft thought, that may difparage me ;
Yet when *fuch men* as *I*, fhall haue *fuch foes*,
Accufe me of *fuch crimes*, to *fuch as thofe*,
          Till

A Satyre.

Till I had meanes my *Innocence* to fhow,
Their *Iuſtice* could haue done no leſſe then ſo.
    Nor haue I ſuch a proud conceited wit,
Or felfe-opinion of my knowledge yet,
To thinke it may not be that I haue run
Vpon ſome *Errors* in what I haue done,
Worthy this puniſhment which I endure;
(I ſay I cannot ſo my felfe aſſure)
For 'tis no wonder if their *Wifedomes* can
Difcouer *Imperfections* in a man
So weake as I, (more then himfelfe doth ſee)
Since my *fight* dull with *infufficiencie*,
In men more graue, and wifer farre then I,
Innumerable *Errors* doth eſpye,
Which they with all their knowledge I'le be bold,
Cannot (or will not) in themſelues behold.
But ere I will *my ſelfe* accuſe my *Song*,
Or keepe a *Tongue* ſhall doe my *Heart* that wrong,
To ſay I willingly in what I penn'd,
Did ought that might a *Goodmans* fight offend;
Or with my knowledge did infert one word,
That might difparage a true *Honour'd Lord*;
Let it be in my mouth a helpeleſſe ſore,
And neuer ſpeake to be beleeued more.
    Yet *man* irrefolute is, vnconſtant, weake,
And doth his purpoſe oft through frailty breake.
Left therefore I by force hereafter may
Be brought from this minde, and theſe words vnſay,

Here

A Satyre.

Here to the *World* I doe proclaime before,
If e're my refolution be fo poore,
T'is not the *Right*, but *Might* that makes me doe it;
Yea, nought but *fearefull bafeneffe* brings me to it;
Which if I ftill hate, as I now deteft,
Neuer can come to harbor in my breft.
 Thus my fault then (if they a fault imply)
Is not alone an ill vnwillingly,
But alfo, might I know it, I entend,
Not onely to acknowledge, but amend :
Hoping that *thou* wilt not be fo feuere,
To punifh me aboue all other here.
But for m'intents fake, and my loue to *Truth*,
Impute my *Errors* to the heate of *Youth*,
Or rather *Ignorance*; then to my *Will*,
Which fure I am was *good*, what e're be *ill*,
And like to him now, in whofe place thou art,
What e're the refidue be, accept the *Heart*.
But I grow tedious, and my loue abusd,
Difturbs my thoughts, and makes my lines confus'd.
Yet pardon me, and daigne a gracious eye
On this my rude, vnfil'd *Apologie*.
Let not the bluntneffe of my phrafe offend,
Weigh but the *matter*, and not how 'tis *penn'd*;
By thefe abrupt lines in my iuft defence,
Iudge what I might fay for my innocence.
*And thinke, I more could fpeake, that here I fpare,
Becaufe my power fuites not to what I dare.*
           My

A Satyre.

My vnaffected *ſtile* retaines (you ſee)
Her old *Frize-Cloake* of young *Ruſticitie* :
If others will vſe neater tearmes, they may,
Ruder I am, yet loue as well as they :
And *(though if I would ſmooth't I cannot doo't)*
My humble heart I bend beneath thy foot :
While here my Muſe her diſcontent doth ſing
To thee her great *Apollo*, and my *King :*
Emploring thee by that high ſacred *Name*,
By *Iuſtice*, by thoſe *Powers* that I could name :
By whatſoe're may moue, entreate I *thee*,
To be what thou art vnto all, to mee ;
I feare it not, yet giue me leaue to pray,
I may haue foes, whoſe power doth beare ſuch ſway ;
If they but ſay I'me guilty of offence,
'Twere vaine for me to pleade my innocence.
   But as the Name of God thou bear'ſt, I truſt
Thou imitat'ſt him to, in being iuſt :
That when the right of *Truth* thou comm'ſt to ſcan,
Thoul't not reſpect the perſon of the man :
For if thou doe, then is my hope vndone,
The head-long-way to ruine I muſt runne.
For whil'ſt that they haue all the helpes which may
Procure their pleaſure with my ſoone decay :
How is it like that I my peace can win me,
When all the ayde I haue, comes from within me ?
Therefore *(good King)* that mak'ſt thy bounty ſhine
Sometime on thoſe whoſe worths are ſmall as mine ;
                                           Oh

A Satyre.

Oh saue me now from Enuies *dangerous shelfe,*
Or make me able, and I'le saue my selfe.
Let not the want of that make me a scorne,
To which there are more *Fooles* then *Wise-men* borne.
Let me not for my *Meannesse* be dispis'd,
Nor others *greatnesse* make their words more priz'd.
For whatsoe're my outward *Fate* appeares,
My *Soule*'s as good, my *Heart* as great as theirs.
My loue vnto my *Country* and to *thee*,
As much as his that more would seeme to be.
And would this Age allow but meanes to show it,
Those that misdoubt it, should ere long time know it.
    Pitty my youth then, and let me not lie
Wasting my time in fruitlesse miserie.
Though I am meane, I may be borne vnto
That seruice, which another cannot doe.
In vaine the little Mouse the Lyon spar'd not,
She did him pleasure, when a greater dar'd not.
If ought that I haue done, doe *thee* displease,
Thy misconceiued wrath I will appease,
Or sacrifice my heart; but why should I
Suffer for God knowes whom, I know not why?
If that my words through *some* mistake offends,
Let them conceiue them right and make amends.
Or were I guilty of offence indeed,
One fault (they say) *doth but one pardon need*:
Yet one I had, and now I want one more;
For once I stood accus'd for this before.

                                                  As

A Satyre.

As I remember I fo long agon,
Snng *Thame*, and *Rhynes Epithalamion*:
When SHE that from thy Royall felfe deriues
Thofe gracious vertues that beft *Title* giues:
She that makes *Rhine* proud of her excellence,
And me oft minde her reuerence;
Daign'd in her *great good-nature* to encline
Her gentle care to fuch a caufe as mine;
And which is more, vouchfaf'd her word, to cleare
Me from all dangers (if there any were,)
So that I doe not now intreate, or fue
For any great boone, or requeft that's new:
But onely this *(*though abfent from the Land*)*
Her former fauour ſtill in force might ſtand:
And that her word (who preſent was ſo deere)
Might be as powerfull, as when ſhe was here.
Which if I finde, and with thy fauour may
Haue leaue to ſhake my loathed *bands* away,
(As I doe hope I ſhall*)* and be fet free
From all the troubles, this hath brought on me,
I'le make her *Name* giue life vnto a *Song*,
Whofe neuer-dying note ſhall laſt as long
As there is either *Riuer*, *Groue* or *Spring*,
Or *Downe* for *Sheepe*, or *Shepheards Lad* to fing.
Yea, I will teach my *Mufe* to touch a ſtraine,
That was ne're reach't to yet by any *Swaine*.
For though that many deeme my yeeres vnripe,
Yet I haue learn'd to tune an Oaten Pipe,
                                        Whereon

A Satyre.

Whereon I'le try what muficke I can make me,
(Vntill *Bellona* with her Trumpe awake me.)
And fince the world will not haue *Vice* thus fhowne,
By blazing *Vertue* I will make it knowne.
Then if the *Court* will not my lines approue
I'le goe vnto fome *Mountaine*, or thicke *Groue* :
There to my fellow *Shepheards* will I fing,
Tuning my *Reede* vnto fome dancing *Spring*,
In fuch a note, that none fhould dare to trouble it,
Till the *Hils* anfwere, and the *Woods* redouble it.
And peraduenture I may then goe neare
To fpeake of fomething thoul't be pleas'd to heare :
And that which *thofe* who now my tunes abhorre,
Shall reade, and like, and daigne to loue me for :
But the meane while, oh paffe not this fuite by,
Let thy *free hand* figne me my *liberty* :
And if my loue may moue thee more to do,
Good King confider this my trouble to.
Others haue found thy fauour in diftreffe,
Whofe loue to thee and thine I thinke was leffe.
And I might fitter for thy *feruice liue*
On what would not be much for *thee* to giue.
   And yet I aske it not for that I feare
The outward meanes of life fhould faile me here :
For though I want to compaffe thofe *good ends*
I aime at for my *Countrie* and my *Friends*,
In this *poore ftate* I can as well content me,
As if that I had *Wealth* and *Honours* lent me,
                                              Nor

A Satyre.

Nor for my *owne sake* doe I seeke to shunne
This *thraldome*, wherein now I seeme vndone:
For though I prize my *Freedome* more then *Gold*,
And vse the meanes to free my selfe from hold,
Yet with a minde (I hope) vnchang'd and free,
Here can I liue, and play with miserie:
Yea, in despight of want and slauerie,
Laugh at the world in all her brauerie.
Here haue I learn'd to make my greatest Wrongs
Matter of Mirth, *and subiects but for* Songs:
Here can I smile to see my selfe neglected,
And how the meane mans suite is dis-respected;
Whil'st those that are more rich, and better friended,
Can haue twice greater faults *thrice sooner ended.*
 All this, yea more, I see and suffer to,
Yet liue content midst discontents I do.
Which whil'st I can, it is all one to me,
Whether in *Prison* or *abroad* it be:
For should I still lye here *distrest* and *poore*,
It shall not make me breathe a sigh the more;
Since to my selfe it is indifferent,
Where the small remnant of my daies be spent,
But for *Thy* sake, my *Countries*, and my *Friends*,
For whom, more then my selfe, *God* this life lends,
I would not, could I helpe it, be a scorne,
But (if I might) liue free, as I was borne:
Or rather for my Mistris *vertues* sake,
Faire Vertue, of whom most account I make,

If

A Satyre.

If I can chufe, I will not be debas'd
In this laft action, left She *be difgrac'd:*
For 'twas the loue of her that brought me to,
What *Spleene* nor *Enuie* could not make me do.
And if her *feruants* be no more regarded;
If enemies of *Vice* be thus rewarded,
And I fhould alfo *Vertues* wrongs conceale,
And if none liu'd to whom fhe dar'd appeale:
Will they that doe not yet her *worth* approue,
Be euer drawne to entertaine her *loue*,
When they fhall fee him plagu'd as an *Offender*,
Who for the loue he beares her, doth commend her?
    This may to others more offenfiue be,
Then preiudiciall any way to me:
For who will his endeauours euer bend
To follow her, whom there is none will friend?
Some I doe hope there be that nothing may
From loue of *Truth* and *Honefty* difmay.
But who will (that fhall fee my euill *Fortune*)
The *remedy* of *Times Abufe* importune?
Who will againe, when they haue fmother'd me,
Dare to oppofe the face of *Villany?*
Whereas he muft be faine to vndertake
A *Combat* with a fecond *Lernean* Snake;
Whofe euer-growing heads when as he crops,
Not onely two fprings, for each one he lops,
But alfo he fhall fee in midft of dangers,
Thofe he thought *friends* turne *foes*, at leaft-wife *ftrangers*.
                                          More

A Satyre.

More I could fpeake, but fure if this doe faile me,
I neuer fhall doe ought that will auaile me;
Nor care to fpeake againe, vnleffe it be
To him that knowes how *heart* and *tongue agree*;
No, nor to liue, when none dares vndertake
To fpeake one word for honeft *Vertues* fake.
But let *his will be done*, that beft knowes what
Will be my *future* good, and what will not.
Hap *well* or *ill*, my fpotleffe *meaning*'s faire,
And for *thee*, this fhall euer be my prayer,
*That thou maift here enioy a long-bleft Raigne,
And dying, be in Heauen re-crown'd againe.*

SO now, if thou haft daign'd my *Lines* to heare,
There's nothing can befall *me* that I feare:
For if *thou* haft compaffion on my trouble,
The *Ioy* I fhall receiue will be made double;
And if I fall, it may fome *Glory* be,
That none but I O V E *himfelfe did ruine me.*

Your Maiefties *moft loyall Subiect,
and yet Prifoner in the Marfhalfey,*

GEORGE WITHER.

Epithalamia:
OR
NVPTIALL POEMS
VPON THE MOST BLESSED
AND HAPPY MARRIAGE
betweene the High and Mighty Prince
Frederick *the fifth, Count Palatine*
of the Rhine, Duke of
Bauier, &c.

AND THE MOST VERTVOVS,
Gracious, and thrice Excellent Princeffe, *Elizabeth,*
Sole Daughter to our dread Soueraigne, Iames, *by*
the grace of God King of Great *Britaine,*
France and *Ireland,* Defender of
the Faith, &c.

Celebrated at *White-Hall* the fourteenth
of February. 1612.

Written by George Wither.

LONDON,
Printed by *T. S.* for *Iohn Budge,* dwelling in *Pauls-*
Church-yard, at the figne of the Greene
Dragon, 1622.

TO THE ALL-VER-
TVOVS AND THRICE
EXCELLENT PRINCESSE

Elizabeth, fole daughter to our dread
Soueraigne, Iames *by the grace of*
God, King of *Great Britaine*,
France and *Ireland*,
&c.

AND WIFE TO THE HIGH
AND MIGHTY PRINCE, FREDERICK
the fifth, Count Palatine of the *Rheine*, Duke
of *Bauier*, *&c. Elector, and Arch-few er to*
the facred Roman Empire, during
the vacancy Vicar of the fame,
and Knight of the moft hono-
rable Order of the
Garter.

George Wither wifheth all the Health;
Ioyes, Honours, and Felicities of this World,
in this life, and the perfections of eternity
in the World to come.

To the Christian Readers.

*R*Eaders; *for that in my booke of* Satyricall Essayes, *I haue been deemed ouer* Cynicall; *to shew, that I am not wholly inclined to that* Vaine: *But indeede especially, out of the loue which in duty I owe to those incomparable* Princes, *I haue in honour of their* Royall Solemnities, *published these short* Epithalamiaes. *By which you may perceiue (how euer the world thinke of me) I am not of such a* Churlish Constitution, *but I can afford* Vertue *her deserued honour; and haue as well an*

Ff 4 *affable*

To the Reader.

affable looke to encourage Honesty; *as a sterne frowne to cast on* Villanie; *If the* Times *would suffer me, I could be as pleasing as others; and perhaps ere long I will make you amends for my former rigor; Meane while I commit this vnto your censures; and bid you farewell.*

G. W.

Epithalamion.

Right *Northerne* Starre, and great *Mineruaes*
   peere,
Sweete *Lady* of this *Day*: Great *Britaines*
   deere.
   Loe thy poore *Vaſſall*, that was erſt ſo rude,
With his moſt *Ruſticke Satyrs* to intrude,
Once more like a poore *Siluan* now drawes neare;
And in thy ſacred *Preſence* dares appeare.
Oh let not that ſweete *Bowe* thy *Brow* be bent,
To ſcarre him with a *Shaft* of diſcontent:
One looke with *Anger*, nay thy gentleſt *Frowne*,
Is twice enough to caſt a *Greater* downe.
My *Will* is euer, neuer to offend,
Theſe that are good; and what I here intend,
Your *Worth* compels me to. For lately greeu'd,
More then can be expreſt, or well beleeu'd;
Minding for euer to abandon ſport,
And liue exilde from places of reſort;
Careleſſe of all, I yeelding to ſecuritie,
Thought to ſhut vp my *Muſe* in darke obſcuritie:
                                          And

Epithalamia.

And in content, the better to repofe,
A lonely *Groue* vpon a *Mountaine* chofe.
Eaft from *Caer Winn*, mid-way twixt *Arle* and *Dis*,
True *Springs*, where *Britains* true *Arcadia* is.
But ere I entred my entended courfe,
Great *Æolus* began to offer force.

<small>* He here remembers and defcribes the late Winter, which was fo exceeding tempeftuous and windy.</small>

* The boifterous *King* was growne fo mad with rage ;
That all the Earth, was but his furies ftage.
Fire, *Ayre*, *Earth*, *Sea*, were intermixt in one :
Yet *Fire*, through *Water*, *Earth* and *Ayre* fhone.
The *Sea*, as if fhe ment to whelme them vnder,
Beat on the *Cliffes*, and rag'd more loud then thunder :
And whil'ft the *vales* fhe with falt waues did fill,
The *Aire* fhowr'd *flouds*, that drencht our higheft hill ;
And the proud trees, that would no dutie know ;
Lay ouer-turned, twenties in a Row.
Yea, euery Man for feare, fell to *Deuotion* ;
Left the whole *Ile* fhould haue bin drencht in th'Ocean.
Which I perceiuing, coniur'd vp my *Mufe*,
The *Spirit*, whofe good helpe I fometime vfe :
And though I ment to breake her reft no more,
I was then faine her aide for to implore.
And by her helpe indeed, I came to know,
Why, both the *Ayre* and *Seas* were troubled fo.
For hauing vrg'd her, that fhe would vnfold
What caufe fhe knew : Thus much at laft fhe told.
Of late (quoth fhe) *there is by powers Diuine* ;
A match concluded, twixt Great Thame *and* Rhine.

Two

Epithalamia.

Two famous Riuers, *equall both to* Nile :
The one, the pride of Europes *greateſt Ile.*
Th'other diſdaining to be cloſely pent ;
Waſhes a great part of the Continent.
Yet with abundance, doth the Wants *ſupply,*
Of the ſtill-thirſting Sea, *that's neuer dry.*
And now, theſe, *being not alone endear'd,*
To mightie Neptune, *and his watrie* Heard :
But alſo to the great and dreadfull Ioue,
With all his ſacred Companies aboue,
Both haue aſſented by their Loues *inuiting* :
To grace (with their owne preſence) this Vniting.
Ioue *call'd a* Summons *to the* Worlds *great wonder,*
'Twas that we heard of late, which we thought thunder. <small>The reaſon of the tempeſtuous Winter.</small>
A thouſand Legions *he intends to ſend them,*
Of Cherubins *and* Angels *to attend them* :
And thoſe ſtrong Windes, *that did ſuch bluſtring keepe,*
Were but the Tritons, *ſounding in the* Deepe ;
To warne each Riuer, *petty* Streame *and* Spring,
Their aide vnto their Soueraigne *to bring.*
The Floods *and* Showres *that came ſo plenteous downe,*
And lay entrencht in euery Field *and* Towne,
Were but retainers to the Nobler ſort,
That owe their Homage at the Watrie Court :
Or elſe the Streames *not pleaſ'd with their owne ſtore,*
To grace the Thames, *their* Miſtris, *borrowed more.*
Exacting from their neighbouring Dales *and* Hills,
But by conſent all (nought againſt their wills.)
                                                    Yet

Epithalamia.

Yet now, since in this stirre are brought to ground
Many faire buildings, many hundreds drown'd,
And daily found of broken Ships great store,
That lie dismembred vpon euery shore:
With diuers other mischiefes knowne to all,
This is the cause that those great harmes befall.
Whilst other, things in readinesse, did make,

<small>The cause of all such dangers as fall out during the distemperature of the ayre.</small> *Hells hatefull Hags from out their prisons brake:*
And spighting at this hopefull match, began
To wreake their wrath on Ayre, Earth, Sea, *and* Man.
Some hauing shapes of Romish *shauelings got,*
Spew'd out their venome; and began to plot
Which way to thwart it: others made their way
With much distraction thorough Land *and* Sea
Extreamely raging. But Almightie Ioue
Perceiues their Hate *and* Enuie *from aboue:*
He'le checke their furie, and in yrons chain'd,
Their libertie abus'd, shall be restrain'd:
Hee'le shut them vp, from comming to molest
The Meriments of Hymens *holy feast.*
Where shall be knit that sacred Gordian *knot,*
Which in no age to come shall be forgot.
Which Policie *nor* Force *shall nere vntie,*
But must continue to eternitie:
Which for the whole Worlds *good was fore-decree'd,*
With Hope *expected long; now come indeed.*
And of whose future glory, worth, *and* merit
Much I could speake with a prophetike spirit.

             Thus

Epithalamia.

Thus by my *Muses* deare affiftance, finding
The caufe of this difturbance, with more minding   *He noteth the moft admirable alteration of the weather a while before thefe Nuptials.*
My Countries welfare, then my owne content,
And longing to behold this *Tales* euent:
My lonely life I fuddenly forfooke,
And to the *Court* againe my Iourney tooke.
   Meane-while I faw the furious *Windes* were laid;
The rifings of the fwelling *Waters* ftaid.
The *Winter* gan to change in euery thing,
And feem'd to borrow mildneffe of the *Spring*.
The *Violet* and *Primrofe* frefh did grow;
And as in *Aprill*, trim'd both *Cops* and *rowe*.
The *Citie*, that I left in mourning clad,
Drouping, as if it would haue ftill beene fad,
I found deckt vp in roabes fo neat and trimme,
Faire *Iris* would haue look't but ftale and dimme
In her beft colours, had fhe there appear'd,
The *Sorrowes* of the *Court* I found well cleer'd,
Their wofull habits quite caft off, and ty'rd
In fuch a glorious fafhion: I admir'd.   *The glorious preparation, of this folemnity, the ftate whereof is here allegorically defcribed.*
All her chiefe *Peeres* and choifeft *beauties* to,
In greater pompe, then *Mortals* vfe to doe,
Wait as attendants. *Iuno*'s come to fee;
Becaufe fhe heares that this folemnitie
Exceeds faire *Hippodamia's* (where the ftrife
'Twixt *her, Minerua,* and lame *Vulcans* wife
Did firft arife,) and with her leades along
A noble, ftately, and a mighty throng.
                                    Venus

Epithalamia.

Venus, (attended with her rareſt features,
Sweet louely-ſmiling, and heart-mouing creatures,
The very faireſt *Iewels* of her treaſure,
Able to moue the ſenceles ſtones to pleaſure.)
Of all her ſweeteſt *Saints*, hath robd their ſhrines ;
And brings them for the Courtiers *Valentines.*
Nor doth Dame *Pallas*, from theſe triumphs lurke ;
Her nobleſt wits, ſhe freely ſets on worke.
Of late ſhe ſummond them vnto this place,
To doe your maskes and *Reuels* better grace.

[*] Meaning the Sea-fight, and the taking of the Caſtle on the water, which was moſt artificially performed.

Here * *Mars* himſelfe to, clad in Armour bright,
Hath ſhowne his furie in a bloudleſſe fight ;
And both on land and water, ſternely dreſt,
Acted his bloudy *Stratagems* in ieſt :
Which (to the people, frighted by their error,)
With ſeeming wounds and death did ad more terror,
Beſides, to giue the greater cauſe of wonder,
Ioue did vouchſafe a ratling peale of thunder :

The fier-workes he alludeth to thoſe exhalations.

Comets and *Meteors* by the ſtarres exhald,
Were from the *Middle-Region* lately cald ;
And to a place appointed made repaire,
To ſhow their fierie Friſcols in the aire,
People innumerable doe reſort,
As if all *Europe* here would keepe one Court :
Yea, *Hymen* in his Safferon-coloured weed,
To celebrate his rites is full agreed.
All this I ſee : which ſeeing, makes me borrow
Some of their mirth a while, and lay downe ſorrow.

And

Epithalamia.

And yet not this: but rather the delight
My heart doth take in the much hoped fight
Of thefe thy glories, long already due;
And this fweet comfort, that my eyes doe view
Thy happy Bridegroome, *Prince Count Palatine*,
Now thy beft friend and trueft *Valentine*.
Vpon whofe brow, my minde doth reade the ftorie
Of mightie *fame*, and a true future glorie.
Me thinkes I doe forefee already, how
Princes and *Monarchs* at his ftirrop bow:
I fee him fhine in fteele; the bloudy fields
Already won, and how his proud *foe* yeelds.
God hath ordaind him happineffe great ftore:
And yet in nothing is he happy more,
Then in thy loue (faire *Princeffe*:) For (vnleffe
Heauen, like to *Man*, be prone to fickleneffe)
Thy *Fortunes* muft be greater in effect,
Then *time* makes fhow of, or *men* can expect.
Yet, notwithftanding all thofe goods of *fate*,
Thy *Minde* fhall euer be aboue thy *ftate:*
For ouer and befide thy proper merit,
Our laft *Eliza* grants her Noble fpirit
To be re-doubled on thee; and your *names*
Being both one, fhall giue you both one fames.
Oh bleffed thou! and they to whom thou giu'ft
The leaue for to be attendants where thou liu'ft:
And hapleffe we, that muft of force let goe,
The matchleffe treafure we efteeme of fo.

                                                      But

Epithalamia.

But yet we truſt 'tis for our good and thine;
Or elſe thou ſhouldſt not change thy *Thame* for *Rhyne.*
We hope that this will the vniting proue
Of *Countries* and of *Nations* by your *loue:*
And that from out your bleſſed loynes, ſhall come
Another terror to the *Whore of Rome*:
And ſuch a ſtout *Achilles,* as ſhall make
Her tottering Walls and weake foundation ſhake:
For *Thetis*-like, thy fortunes doe require,
Thy *Iſſue* ſhould be greater then his *ſire.*
But (*Gracious Princeſſe*) now ſince thus it fares,
And God ſo well for you and vs prepares:
Since he hath daign'd ſuch honours for to doe you,
And ſhowne himſelfe ſo fauourable to you:
Since he hath chang'd your ſorrowes, and your ſadnes,
Into ſuch great and vnexpected gladneſſe:
Oh now remember you to be at leaſure,
Sometime to thinke on him amidſt your pleaſure:
Let not theſe glories of the *world* deceaue you,
Nor her vaine fauours of your ſelfe bereaue you.
Conſider yet for all this Iollitie,
Y'are mortall, and muſt feele mortalitie:
And that God can in midſt of all your Ioyes,
Quite daſh this pompe, and fill you with annoyes.
Triumphes are fit for *Princes*; yet we finde
They ought not wholly to take vp the minde,
Nor yet to be let paſſe; as things in vaine:
For out of all things, wit will knowledge gaine.

Muſique

Epithalamia.

Mufique may teach of difference in degree,
The beſt tun'd *Common-Weales* will framed bee:
And that he moues, and liues with greateſt grace,
That vnto *Time* and *Meaſure* ties his pace.
Then let theſe things be ᵃ *Emblemes*, to preſent
Your minde with a more laſting true content.
When you behold the infinite reſort,
The glory and the ſplendor of the Court;
What wondrous fauours God doth here bequeath you,
How many hundred thouſands are beneath you;
And view with admiration your great bliſſe,
Then with your ſelfe you may imagine this.
'Tis but a blaſt, or tranſitory ſhade,
Which in the turning of a hand may fade.
Honours, which you your ſelfe did neuer winne,
And might (had God been pleas'd) anothers binne.
And thinke, if ſhadowes haue ſuch maieſtie,
What are the glories of eternitie;
Then by this image of a *fight on Sea*,
Wherein you heard the thundring Canons plea;
And ſaw flames breaking from their murthering throts,
Which in true skirmiſh, fling reſiſtleſſe ſhots;
Your wiſedome may (and will no doubt) begin,
To caſt what perill a poore *Souldiers* in:
You will conceaue his miſeries and cares,
How many dangers, deaths, and wounds he ſhares:
Then though the moſt paſs't ouer, and neglect them,
That *Rethoricke* will moue you to reſpect them.

ᵃ He declares what vſe is to be made of theſe ſhowes and triumphes, and what meditations the minde may be occupied about, when we behold them.

Epithalamia.

And if hereafter, you fhould hap to fee
Such *Mimick Apes* (that Courts difgraces be:)
I meane fuch Chamber-combatants; who neuer
Weare other Helmet, then a Hat of *Beuer*:
Or nere board *Pinnace* but in filken faile;
And in the fteed of boyfterous fhirts of maile,
Goe arm'd in *Cambrick*: If that fuch a *Kite*
(I fay) fhould fcorne an *Eagle* in your fight;
Your *wifedome* iudge (by this experience) can,
Which hath moft worth, *Hermaphrodite*, or *Man*.
* Fire-workes. The *nights* ftrange * profpects, made to feed the eies,
With Artfull fiers, mounted in the skies:
Graced with horred claps of fulphury thunders;
May make you minde th'Almighties greater wonders.
Nor is there any thing, but you may thence
Reape inward gaine; as well as pleafe the *Senfe*.
But pardon me (*oh faireft*) that am bold,
My heart thus freely, plainely, to vnfold.
What though I know, you knew all this before:
My loue *this* fhowes, and that is fomething more.
Doe not my honeft feruice here difdaine,
I am a faithfull, though an humble Swaine.
I'me none of thofe that haue the meanes or place,
With fhowes of coft to doe your *Nuptials* grace:
But onely mafter of mine owne defire,
Am hither come with others to admire.
I am not of thofe *Heliconian* wits;
Whofe pleafing ftraines the *Courts* knowne humour fits.
But

Epithalamia.

But a poore rurall *Shepheard*, that for need,
Can make fheepe Mufique on an *Oaten* reed:
Yet for my *loue* (Ile this be bold to boaft)
It is as much to you, as his that's moft.
Which, fince I no way elfe can now explaine,
If you'l in midft of all thefe *glories* daigne,
To lend your eares vnto my *Mufe* fo long,
She fhall declare it in a *Wedding fong*.

Epithalamion.

<small>The Marriage being on S. Valentines day, the Author fhowes it by beginning with the falutation of a fuppofed Valentine.</small>

V*Alentine*, good morrow to thee,
Loue and feruice both I owe thee:
And would waite vpon thy pleafure;
But I cannot be at leafure:
For, I owe this *day* as debter,
To (a thoufand times) thy better.

Hymen now will haue effected
What hath been fo long expected:
Thame thy *Miftris*, now vnwedded;
Soone, muft with a *Prince* be bedded.
If thou'lt fee her *Virgin* euer,
Come, and doe it now, or neuer.

Where art thou, oh faire *Aurora?*
Call in *Ver* and Lady *Flora*:
And you daughters of the *Morning*,
In your neat'ft, and feat'ft adorning:
Cleare your fore-heads, and be fprightfull,
That this *day* may feeme delightfull.

All

Epithalamia.

All you *Nimphs* that vſe the Mountaines,
Or delight in groues and fountaines ;
Shepheardeſſes, you that dally,
Either vpon Hill or Valley :
And you daughters of the *Bower*,
That acknowledge *Veſtaes* power.

Oh you ſleepe too long ; awake yee,
See how *Time* doth ouertake yee.
Harke, the *Larke* is vp and ſingeth,
And the houſe with ecchoes ringeth.
Pretious howers, why negleƈt yee,
Whil'ſt affaires thus expeƈt yee ?

Come away vpon my bleſſing,
The *Bride-chamber* lies to dreſſing :
Strow the wayes with leaues of *Roſes*,
Some make *garlands*, ſome make *poſes* :
'Tis a fauour, and't may ioy you,
That your *Miſtris* will employ you.

Where's ᵃ *Sabrina*, with her daughters,   *a* Seuerne.
That doe ſport about her waters :
Thoſe that with their lockes of *Amber*,
Haunt the fruitfull hills of ᵇ Camber :   *b* Wales.
We muſt haue to fill the number,
All the *Nimphs* of *Trent* and *Humber*.

Epithalamia.

Fie, your hafte is fcarce fufficing,
For the *Bride*'s awake and rifing.
Enter beauties, and attend her ;
All your helpes and feruice lend her :
With your quaint'ft and new'ft deuifes,
Trim your Lady, faire *Thamifis.*

See ; fhee's ready : with *Ioyes* greet her,
Lads, goe bid the *Bride-groome* meet her :
But from rafh approach aduife him,
Left a too much Ioy furprize him,
None I ere knew yet, that dared,
View an *Angell* vnprepared.

Now vnto the *Church* fhe hies her ;
Enuie burfts, if fhe efpies her :
In her geftures as fhe paces,
Are vnited all the *Graces* :
Which who fees and hath his fenfes,
Loues in fpight of all defences.

O moft true maieftick creature !
Nobles did you note her feature ?
Felt you not an inward motion,
Tempting *Loue* to yeeld deuotion ;
And as you were euen defiring,
Something check you for afpiring ?
                              That's

Epithalamia.

That's her *Vertue* which ſtill tameth
Looſe deſires, and bad thoughts blameth:
For whil'ſt others were vnruly,
She obſeru'd *Diana* truly:
And hath by that meanes obtained
Gifts of her that none haue gained.

Yon's the *Bride-groome*, d'yee not ſpie him?
See how all the *Ladies* eye him.
Venus his perfection findeth,
And no more *Adonis* mindeth.
Much of him my heart diuineth:
On whoſe brow all *Vertue* ſhineth.

Two ſuch *Creatures Nature* would not
Let one place long keepe: ſhe ſhould not:
One ſhee'l haue (ſhe cares not whether,)
But our *Loues* can ſpare her neither.
Therefore ere we'le ſo be ſpighted,
They in one ſhall be vnited.

Natures ſelfe is well contented,
By that meanes to be preuented.
And behold they are retired,
So conioyn'd, as we deſired:
Hand in hand, not onely fixed,
But their hearts, are intermixed.

Epithalamia.

Happy they and we that fee it,
For the good of *Europe* be it.
And heare *Heauen* my deuotion,
Make this *Rhyne* and *Thame* an *Ocean*:
That it may with might and wonder,
Whelme the pride of ᵃ *Tyber* vnder.

<small>ᵃ Tyber is the Riuer which runneth by Rome.</small>

<small>ᵇ White-Hall.</small>

Now yon ᵇ *Hall* their perfons fhroudeth,
Whither all this people croudeth :
There they feafted are with plenty,
Sweet *Ambrofia* is no deinty.
Groomes quaffe *Nectar* ; for theres meeter,
Yea, more coftly wines and fweeter.

Young men all, for ioy goe ring yee,
And your merrieft *Carols* fing yee.
Here's of *Damzels* many choices,
Let them tune their fweeteft voyces.
Fet the *Mufes* to, to cheare them ;
They can rauifh all that heare them.

Ladies, 'tis their *Highneffe* pleafures,
To behold you foot the *Meafures* :
Louely geftures addeth graces,
To your bright and *Angell* faces.
Giue your actiue mindes the bridle :
Nothing worfe then to be idle.

Worthies

Epithalamia.

Worthies, your affaires forbeare yee,
For the *State* a while may fpare yee :
Time was, that you loued fporting,
Haue you quite forgot your Courting ?
Ioy the heart of *Cares* beguileth :   *Semel*
Once a yeere Apollo *fmileth.*   *in an-*
                                                        no ri-
                                                        det
                                                        Apol.

Fellow Shepheards, how I pray you,
Can your *flocks* at this time ftay you ?
Let vs alfo hie vs thither,
Let's lay all our wits together,
And fome *Paftorall* inuent them,
That may fhow the *loue* we ment them.

I my felfe though meaneft ftated,
And in *Court* now almoft hated,
Will knit vp my ᵃ *Scourge*, and venter   *a* Abufes
In the midft of them to enter ;   ftript
                                                        and
For I know, there's no difdaining,   whipt.
Where I looke for entertaining.   He no-
                                                        teth the
                                                        mildneffe
                                                        of the
                                                        winter
                                                        which,
See, me thinkes the very *feafon*,   excep-
                                                        ting that
As if capable of Reafon,   the be-
                                                        ginning
Hath laine by her natiue rigor,   was very
                                                        windy,
The faire *Sun-beames* haue more vigor.   was as
                                                        tempe-
They are *Æols* moft endeared :   rate as
                                                        the
For the *Ayre's* ftill'd and cleared.   fpring.

                                       Fawnes

Epithalamia.

Fawnes, and *Lambs* and *Kidds* doe play,
In the honour of this *day* :
The fhrill *Black-Bird*, and the *Thrufh*
Hops about in euery bufh :
And among the tender twigs,
Chaunt their fweet harmonious ijgs.

<small>Moft men are of o-pinion, that this day euery bird doth chufe her mate for that yeer.</small> Yea, and mou'd by this example,
They doe make each *Groue* a *temple* :
Where their *time* the beft way vfing,
They their *Summer loues* are chufing.
And vnleffe fome *Churle* do wrong them,
There's not an od bird among them.

Yet I heard as I was walking,
Groues and hills by *Ecchoes* talking :
Reeds vnto the fmall brooks whiftling,
Whil'ft they danc't with pretty rufhling.
Then for *vs* to fleepe 'twere pitty ;
Since *dumb creatures* are fo witty.

But oh *Titan*, thou doft dally,
Hie thee to thy *Wefterne Valley* :
Let this night one hower borrow :
She fhall pay't againe to morrow :
And if thou'lt that fauor do them,
Send thy fifter *Phæbe* to them.

              But

Epithalamia.

But fhee's come her felfe vnasked,
And brings ᵃ *Gods* and *Heroes* masked.
None yet faw, or heard in ftorie,
Such immortall, mortall glorie.
View not, without *preparation* ;
Left you faint in *admiration.*

ᵃ By thefe he means the two Mafques, one of them being prefented by the Lords, the other by the Gentry.

Say my *Lords*, and fpeake truth barely,
Mou'd they not exceeding rarely ?
Did they not fuch praifes merit,
As if *flefh* had all beene *fpirit ?*
True indeed, yet I muft tell them,
There was *One* did farre excell them.

But (alas) this is ill dealing,
Night vnawares away is ftealing :
Their delay the poore *bed* wrongeth,
That for *Bride* with *Bride-groome* longeth :
And aboue all other places,
Muft be bleft with their embraces.

Reuellers, then now forbeare yee,
And vnto your refts prepare yee :
Let's a while your abfence borrow,
Sleep to night, and *dance* to morrow.
We could well allow your Courting :
But 'twill hinder better fporting.

They

Epithalamia.

They are gone, and *Night* all lonely,
Leaues the *Bride* with *Bridegroome* onely.
Mufe now tell; (for thou haft power
To flie thorough wall or tower : *)*
What contentments their hearts cheareth ;
And how louely fhe appeareth.

And yet doe not; tell it no man,
Rare conceits may fo grow common :
Doe not to the *Vulgar* fhow them,
('Tis enough that *thou* doft know them. *)*
Their ill hearts are but the *Center*,
Where all mifconceiuings enter.

But thou *Luna* that doft lightly,
Haunt our downes and forrefts nightly :
Thou that fauour'ft generation,
And art helpe to procreation :
See their *iſſue* thou fo cherifh,
I may liue to fee it flourifh.

And you *Planets*, in whofe power
Doth confift thefe liues of our ;
You that teach vs *Diuinations*,
Helpe with all your *Conftellations*,
How to frame in *Her*, a creature,
Bleft in *Fortune*, *Wit*, and *Feature*.
                              Laftly,

Epithalamia.

Laftly, oh you *Angels* ward them,
Set your facred *Spels* to gard them;
Chafe away fuch feares or terrors,
As not being, feeme through errors:
Yea, let not a *dreames* molefting,
Make them ftart when they are refting.

But T H O V chiefly, moft adored,
That fhouldft onely be implored:
Thou to whom my meaning tendeth,
Whether er'e in fhow it bendeth:
Let them reft to night from forrow,
And awake with ioy to morrow.

Oh, to my *requeft* be heedfull,
Grant them *that*, and all things needfull.
Let not thefe my ftraines of *Folly*,
Make *true prayer* be vnholy:
But if I haue here offended:
Helpe, forgiue, and fee it mended.

Daigne me *this*. And if my *Mufes*
Haftie iffue; fhe perufes;
Make it vnto her feeme gratefull,
Though to all the *World* elfe hatefull.
But how er'e, yet *Soule* perfeuer
Thus to wifh her good for euer.

Thus

Epithalamia.

THus ends the *Day*, together with my Song;
Oh may the Ioyes thereof continue long!
Let *Heauens* iuſt, all-ſeeing, ſacred power,
Fauour this happy marriage day of your;
And bleſſe you in your chaſt embraces ſo,
We *Britains* may behold before you goe
The hopefull Iſſue we ſhall count ſo deare,
And whom (vnborne) his foes already feare.
Yea, I deſire, that all your ſorrowes may
Neuer be more, then they haue been to day.
Which hoping; for acceptance now I ſue,
And humbly bid your *Grace* and *Court* adue.
I ſaw the ſight I came for; which I know
Was more then all, the world beſide could ſhow.
But if amongſt *Apolloes* Layes, you can
Be pleas'd to lend a gentle eare to *Pan*;
Or thinke your Country *Shepheard* loues as deare,
As if he were a *Courtier*, or a *Peere*:
Then I, that elſe muſt to my *Cell* of paine,
Will ioyfull turne vnto my *flocke* againe:
And there vnto my fellow *ſhepheards* tell,
Why *you* are lou'd; wherein *you* doe excell.
And when we driue our *flocks* a field to graze them,
So chaunt your praiſes, that it ſhall amaze them:
And thinke that *Fate* hath new recald from death
Their ſtill-lamented, ſweete *Elizabeth*.
For though they ſee the *Court* but now and then,
They know *deſert* as well as *Greater* men:
            And

Epithalamia.

And honord *Fame* in them doth liue or die,
As well as in the mouth of *Maieſtie*.
But taking granted what I here intreat;
At heauen for you my *deuotions* beat:
And though I feare, *fate* will not ſuffer me
To doe you ſeruice, where your *Fortunes* be:
How ere my skill hath yet deſpiſed ſeem'd,
(And my vnripened wit been miſeſteem'd:)
When all this coſtly *Showe* away ſhall flit,
And not one liue that doth remember it;
If *Enuies* trouble let not to perſeuer;
I'le find a meanes to make it knowne for euer.

CERTAINE

CERTAINE E-
PIGRAMS CON-
CERNING MAR-
RIAGE.

Epigram 1.

Is *said*; *in Marriage aboue all the rest*
The children of a King finde comforts least,
Because without respect of Loue or Hate
They must, and oft be, ruled by the State:
But *if* contented Loue, Religions care,
Equalitie in State, *and* yeares *declare*
A happie Match (as *I suppose no lesse*)
Then rare and great's Elizaes *Happinesse.*

Epigram

Epithalamia.

Epigram. 2.

GOd *was the first that Marriage did ordaine,*
By making One, Two; and Two, One againe,

Epigram. 3.

SOuldier; *of thee I aske, for thou canst best,*
Hauing knowne sorrow, iudge of Ioy and Rest:
What greater blisse, then after all thy harmes,
To haue a wife that's faire, and lawfull thine;
And lying prison'd 'twixt her Iuory armes,
There tell what thou hast scapt by powers diuine?
How many round thee thou hast murthered seene;
How oft thy soule hath beene neere hand expiring,
How many times thy flesh hath wounded been:
Whil'st she thy fortune, and thy worth admiring,
   With ioy of health, and pitty of thy paine;
   Doth weepe and kisse, and kisse and weepe againe.

Epigram. 4.

FAire Helen *hauing stain'd her husbands bed,*
And mortall hatred 'twixt two Kingdomes bred;
Had still remaining in her so much good,
That Heroes *for her lost their dearest blood:*

Epithalamia.

Then if with all that ill, such worth may last,
Oh what is she worth, that's as faire, and chast!

Epigram. 5.

OLd Orpheus *knew a good* wiues *worth so well,*
That when his dy'd, he followed her to hell,
And for her losse, at the Elizean *Groue,*
He did not onely Ghosts to pitty moue,
But the sad Poet breath'd his sighes so deepe ;
'Tis said, the Diuels could not chuse but weepe.

Epigram. 6.

LOng did I wonder, *and I wonder much,*
Romes Church should from her Clergie take that due:
Thought I, why should she that contentment grutch ?
What, doth she all with continence indue ?
No : But why then are they debar'd that state ?
Is she become a foe vnto her owne ?
Doth she the members of her body hate ?
Or is it for some other cause vnshowne ?
Oh yes : they find a womans lips so dainty ;
They tye themselues from one, caufe they'l haue twenty.

Epigram.

Epithalamia.

Epigram. 7.

WOmen, *as some men say, vnconstant be*;
'Tis like enough, and so no doubt are men:
Nay, if their scapes we could so plainely see,
I feare that scarce there will be one for ten.
  Men haue but their owne lusts that tempt to ill:
Women haue lusts, and mens allurements to:
Alas, if their strengths cannot curbe their will;
What should poore women that are weaker do?
  Oh they had need be chast, and looke about them,
That striue 'gainst lust within, and knaues without them.

FINIS.

THE
SHEPHEARDS
HVNTING:

Being certaine Eglogues written
during the time of the Authors
Imprisonment in the
Marshalsey.

By *George Wither*, Gentleman.

LONDON,
Printed by *T. S.* for *Iohn Budge,* dwelling in *Pauls-*
Church-yard, at the signe of the Greene
Dragon, 1622.

To those Honoured, Noble, and *right Vertuous Friends, my Visi-tants* in the *Marshalsey:*

And to all other my vnknowne Fauourers, who either priuately, or publikely wished me well in my imprisonment.

Oble Friends; you whose vertues made me first in loue with Ver-tue; *and whose worths made mee be thought worthy of your loues: I haue now at last (you see) by Gods assistance, and your encouragement, run through the* Pur-gatorie *of imprisonment; and by the worthy fauour*

To the Reader.

fauour of a iuſt Prince, *ſtand free againe, without the leaſt touch of deiected baſeneſſe. Seeing therefore I was growne beyond my* Hope *ſo fortunate (after acknowledgement of my Creators loue, together with the vnequall'd Clemencie of ſo gracious a Soueraigne) I was troubled to thinke, by what meanes I might expreſſe my thankefulnes to ſo many well-deſeruing friends: No way I found to my deſire, neither yet ability to performe when I found it. But at length conſidering with my ſelfe what you were (that is) ſuch, who fauour honeſty for no ſecond reaſon, but becauſe you yourſelues are good; and ayme at no other reward, but the witneſſe of a ſound conſcience that you doe well, I found, that thankfulneſſe would proue the acceptableſt preſent to ſute with your diſpoſitions; and that I imagined could be no way better expreſſed, then in manifeſting your courteſies, and giuing conſent to your reaſonable demaunds. For the firſt, I confeſſe*

To the Reader.

confeſſe (*with thankes to the diſpoſer of all things, and a true gratefull heart towards you*) *ſo many were the vnexpected Viſitations, and vnhoped kindneſſes receyued, both from ſome among you of my* Acquaintance, *and many other vnknowne* Well-willers *of my Cauſe, that I was perſwaded to entertaine a much better conceit of the* Times, *then I lately conceyued, and aſſured my ſelfe, that* Vertue *had far more followers then I ſuppoſed.*

Somewhat *it diſturbed me to behold our ages* Fauourites, *whilſt they frowned on my honeſt enterpriſes, to take vnto their protections the egregiouſts fopperies: yet much more was my contentment, in that I was reſpected by ſo many of* You, *amongſt whō there are ſome, who can and may as much diſ-eſteeme theſe, as they neglect me: nor could I feare their Malice or Contempt, whilſt I enioyed your fauours, who* (*howſoeuer you are vnder-valued by Fooles for a time*)

ſhall

To the Reader.

shall leaue vnto your posterity so noble a memory, that your names shall be reuerenced by Kings, when many of these who now flourish with a shew of vsurped Greatnesse, *shall eyther weare out of being, or dispoyled of all their patched reputation, grow contemptible in the eyes of their beloued Mistris the* World. *Your* Loue *it is that (enabling me with patience to endure what is already past) hath made me also carefull better to prepare my selfe for all future misaduentures, by bringing to my consideration, what the passion of my iust discontentments had almost quite banished from my remembrance.*

Further, to declare my thankefulnesse, in making apparant my willing minde to be commanded in any seruices of loue, which you shal thinke fit (though I want abilitie to performe great matters) yet I haue according to some of your requests, been contented to giue way to the printing of these Eglogues; *which though it to many seeme*

To the Reader.

ſeeme a ſleight matter, yet being well conſidered of, may prouε a ſtrong argument of my readineſſe to giue you content in a greater matter: for they being (as you well know) begotten with little care, and preſerued with leſſe reſpect, gaue ſufficient euidence, that I meant (rather then any way to deceiue your truſt) to giue the world occaſion of calling my diſcretion in queſtion, as I now aſſure my ſelfe this will: and the ſooner, becauſe ſuch expectations (I perceiue) there are (of I know not what Inuentions) as would haue been fruſtrated, though I had employed the vtmoſt and very beſt of my endeauours.

Notwithſtanding for your ſakes, I haue heere aduentured once againe to make tryall of the Worlds cenſures: and what hath receyued beeing *from your Loues*, I here re-dedicated to *your Worths*, which if your noble diſpoſitions will like well of; or if you will but reaſonably reſpect what your ſelues drew mee vnto, I ſhall be

To the Reader.

be nothing *displeased at others cauils, but resting my selfe contented with your good opinions, scorne all the rabble of vncharitable detractors: For none, I know, will maligne it, except those, who eyther particularly malice my person, or professe themselues enemies to my former Bookes; who (sauing those that were incensed on others speeches) as diuers of you (according to your protestations) haue obserued, are eyther open enemies of our Church; men notoriously guilty of some particular Abuses therein taxt, such malicious* Critickes *who haue the repute of being iudicious, by detracting from others; or at best, such Guls, as neuer approue any thing good, or learned, but eyther that which their shallow apprehensions can apply to the soothing of their owne opinions, or what (indeed rather) they vnderstand not.*

Trust me, how ill soeuer it hath been rewarded, my loue to my Country is inuiolate: my thanke-

To the Reader.

thankefulneſſe to you vnfained, my endeauour to doe euery man good; all my ayme, content with honeſtie: and this my paines (if it may be ſo tearmed) more to auoid idleneſſe, then for affectation of praiſe: and if notwithſtanding all this, I muſt yet not onely reſt my ſelfe content that my innocencie hath eſcaped with ſtrict impriſonment (to the impayring of my ſtate, and hinderance of my fortunes) but alſo be conſtrayned to ſee my guiltleſſe lines, ſuffer the deſpight of ill tongues: yet for my further encouragement, let mee intreate the continuance of your firſt reſpect, wherein I ſhall find that comfort as will be ſufficient to make mee ſet light, and ſo much contemne all the malice of my aduerſaries, that readie to burſt with the venome of their owne hearts, they ſhall ſee

> My Minde enamoured on faire *Vertues* light,
> Tranſcends the limits of their bleared ſight,
> And plac'd aboue their *Enuy* doth contemne,
> Nay, ſit and laugh at, their diſdaine, and them.

But

To the Reader.

But Noble Friends, *I make question neyther of yours, nor any honest mans respect, and therefore will no further vrge it, nor trouble your patience: onely this I le say, that you may not think me too well conceited of my selfe; though the* Time *were to blame, in ill requiting my honest endeauours, which in the eyes of the World deserued better; yet somewhat I am assured there was in me worthy that punishment, which when God shall giue me grace to see and amend, I doubt not but to finde that regard as will be fitting for so much merit as my endeauors may iustly challenge. Meane while, the better to hold my selfe in esteeme with you, and amend the worlds opinion of* Vertue, *I will study to amend my selfe, that I may be yet more worthy to be called*

                       Your Friend,

                          Geo: Wither.

The Shepheards Hunting.

The firſt Eglogue.

THE ARGVMENT.
Willy *leaues his Flocke a while,*
To lament his Friends *exile ;*
Where, though priſon'd, he doth finde,
Hee's ſtill free that's free in Minde :
And that there is no defence
Halfe ſo firme as Innocence.

PHILARETE. WILLIE.

Philarete.

Illy, thou now full *iolly* tun'ſt thy *Reedes,*
Making the *Nymphs* enamor'd on thy ſtrains,
And whilſt thy harmles flock vnscarred feeds,
Haſt the contentment, of hils, groues, & plains :
          Truſt

The Shepheards Hunting.

Truſt me, I *ioy* thou and thy *Muſe* ſo ſpeedes
In ſuch an Age, where ſo much miſchiefe raignes:
   And to my *Care* it ſome redreſſe will be,
   Fortune hath ſo much *grace* to ſmile on thee.

Willy.

To ſmile on me? I nere yet knew her ſmile,
Vnleſſe 'twere when ſhe purpos'd to deceiue me;
Many a *Traine*, and many a *painted Wile*
She caſts, in hope of *Freedome* to bereaue me:
Yet now, becauſe ſhe ſees I ſcorne her guile
To fawne on fooles, ſhe for my *Muſe* doth leaue me.
   And here of late, her wonted *Spite* doth tend,
   To worke me *Care*, by frowning on my *friend*.

Philarete.

Why then I ſee her *Copper-coyne*'s no ſtarling,
'Twill not be *currant* ſtill, for all the guilding)
A *Knaue*, or *Foole*, muſt euer be her *Darling*,
For they haue minds to all occaſions yeelding:
If we get any thing by all our parling.
It ſeemes an *Apple*, but it proues a *Weilding*:
   But let that paſſe: ſweet *Shepheard* tell me this,
   For what beloued *Friend* thy ſorrow is.

Willy.

Art thou, *Philarete*, in durance heere,
And doſt thou aske me for what *Friend* I grieue?
Can I ſuppoſe thy loue to me is deere,
Or this thy *ioy* for my *content* belieue?

                                            When

The Shepheards Hunting.

When thou think'ft thy *cares* touch not me as neere:
Or that I pinne thy *Sorrowes* at my fleeue?
   I haue in thee repofed fo much truft,
   I neuer thought, to find thee fo vniuft.

Philarete.

WIL, why *Willy?* Prethee doe not aske me why?
Doth it diminifh any of thy *care*,
That I in freedome maken *melody*;
And think'ft I cannot as well fomewhat fpare
From my *delight*, to mone thy *mifery*?
'Tis time our *Loues* fhould thefe fufpects forbeare:
Thou art that friend, which thou vnnam'd fhold'ft know,
And not haue drawne my loue in queftion fo.

Philarete.

Forgiue me, and I'le pardon thy miftake,
And fo let this thy *gentle-anger* ceafe,
(I neuer of thy loue will queftion make)
Whilft that the number of our dayes encreafe,
Yet to my felfe I much might feeme to take,
And fomething neere vnto prefumption preafe:
   To thinke me worthy *loue* from fuch a *fpirit*,
   But that I know thy kindneffe paft my merit.

Befides; me thought thou fpak'ft now of a friend,
That feem'd more grieuous difcontents to beare,
Some things I find that doe in fhew offend,
Which to my Patience little trouble are,

The Shepheards Hunting.

And they ere long I hope will haue an end ;
Or though they haue not, much I doe not care :
   So this it was, made me that queſtion moue,
   And not ſuſpect of honeſt *Willies* loue.

Willie.

Alas, thou art exiled from thy Flocke,
And quite beyond the *Deſarts* here confin'd,
Haſt nothing to conuerſe with but a *Rocke* ;
Or at leaſt *Out-lawes* in their *Caues* halfe pin'd :
And do'ſt thou at thy owne miſ-fortune mocke,
Making thy ſelfe to, to thy ſelfe vnkinde?
   When heretofore we talk't we did imbrace :
   But now I ſcarce can come to ſee thy face.

Philarete.

Yet all that *Willy*, is not worth thy ſorrow,
For I haue *Mirth* here thou would'ſt not beleeue,
From deepeſt *cares* the higheſt *ioyes* I borrow.
If ought chance out this day, may make me grieue
I'le learne to mend, or ſcorne it by to morrow.
This barren place yeelds ſomewhat to relieue :
   For, I haue found ſufficient to content me,
   And more true bliſſe then euer freedome lent me.

Willie.

Are *Priſons* then growne places of delight ?
                                      Phil-

The Shepheards Hunting.

Philarete.

'Tis as the *confcience* of the *Prifoner* is,
The very *Grates* are able to affright
The guilty Man, that knowes his deedes amiffe ;
All outward *Pleafures* are exiled quite,
And it is nothing (of it felfe) but this :
  Abhorred loanencffe, darkeneffe, fadneffe, paines,
  Num'n-cold, fharpe-hunger, fchorching thirft and chaines.

Willie.

And thefe are nothing ? ─────────

Philarete.

───────────── Nothing yet to mee.
Onely my friends reftraint is all my *paine.*
And fince I truely find my *confcience* free
From that my *loaneneffe* to, I reape fome gaine.

Willie.

But grant in this no difcontentment be :
It doth thy wifhed liberty reftraine :
And to thy *foule* I thinke there's nothing nearer,
For I could neuer heare thee prize ought dearer.

Philarete.

True, I did euer fet it at a Rate
Too deare for any *Mortals* worth to buy,
'Tis not our greateft *Shepheards* whole eftate,
Shall purchafe from me, my leaft *liberty* :

The Shepheards Hunting.

But I am fubiect to the powers of *Fate*,
And to obey them is no *flauery*:
   They may doe much, but when they haue done all,
   Onely my *body* they may bring in *thrall*.

And 'tis not that (my *Willy*) 'tis my *mind*,
My *mind*'s more precious, freedome I fo weigh
A thoufand wayes they may my *body* bind,
In thoufand *thrals*, but ne're my mind betray:
And thence it is that I *contentment* find,
And beare with *Patience* this my loade away:
   I'me ftill my felfe, and that I'de rather bee,
   Then to be Lord of all *thefe Downes* in fee.

Willie.

Nobly refolu'd, and I doe ioy to hear't,
For 'tis the *minde* of *Man* indeed that's all.
There's nought fo hard but a *braue* heart will bear't,
The *guiltleffe men* count great *afflictions* fmall,
They'le looke on *Death* and *Torment*, yet not fear't,
Becaufe they know *'tis rifing fo to fall*:
   Tyrants may boaft they to much *power* are borne,
   Yet he hath more that *Tyranies* can fcorne.

Philarete.

'Tis right, but I no *Tyranies* endure,
Nor haue I fuffered ought worth name of care
                                  Willie.

The Shepheards Hunting.

Willie.
What e're thou'lt call't, thou may'ſt, but I am ſure,
Many more pine that much leſſe pained are :
Thy looke me thinkes doth ſay thy meaning's pure
And by this paſt I find what thou do'ſt dare :
  But I could neuer yet the *reaſon* know,
  Why thou art lodged in this houſe of wo.

Philarete.
Nor I by *Pan*, nor neuer hope to doe,
But thus it pleaſes ſome ; and I doe gueſſe
Partly a *cauſe* that moues them thereunto,
Which neither will auaile me to expreſſe,
Nor thee to heare, and therefore let it goe,
We muſt not ſay, they doe ſo that oppreſſe :
  Yet I ſhall ne're to ſooth *them* or *the times*,
  Iniure my ſelfe, by bearing others *crimes*.

Willie.
Then now thou maiſt ſpeake freely, there's none heares,
But he, whom I doe hope thou do'ſt not doubt.

Philarete.
True : but if *doores* and *walles* haue gotten *cares*,
And *Cloſet-whiſperings* may be ſpread about :
Doe not blame him that in ſuch *cauſes* feares
What in his *Paſſion* he may blunder out :
  In ſuch a place, and ſuch ſtrict *times* as theſe,
  Where what we ſpeake is tooke as *others* pleaſe.

The Shepheards Hunting.

But yet to morrow, if thou come this way,
I'le tell thee all my ſtory to the end,
'Tis long, and now I feare thou canſt not ſtay,
Becauſe thy Flocke muſt watred be and pend,
And *Night* begins to muffle vp the day,
Which to informe thee how alone I ſpend,
I'le onely ſing a ſorry *Priſoners Lay*,
    I fram'd this *Morne*, which though it ſuits no fields,
    Is ſuch as fits me, and ſad *Thraldome* yeelds.

Willie.

Well, I will ſet my *Kit* another ſtring,
And play vnto it whil'ſt that thou do'ſt ſing.

Sonnet.

Philarete.

Ow that my body dead-aliue,
Bereau'd of comfort, lies in thrall.
Doe thou my ſoule begin to thriue,
And vnto Hony, turne this Gall:
  So ſhall we both through outward wo,
  The way to inward comfort know.

As to the Fleſh we food do giue;
To keepe in vs this Mortall breath:
So, Soules on Meditations liue,
And ſhunne thereby immortall death:

                                Nor

The Shepheards Hunting.

Nor art thou euer neerer rest,
Then when thou find'st me most opprest.

First thinke my Soule; If I haue Foes
That take a pleasure in my care,
And to procure these outward woes,
Haue thus entrapt me vnaware:
  Thou should'st by much more carefull bee,
  Since greater foes lay waite for thee.

Then when Mew'd vp in grates of steele,
Minding those ioyes, mine eyes doe misse,
Thou find'st no torment thou do'st feele,
So grieuous as Priuation is:
  Muse how the Damn'd in flames that glow,
  Pine in the losse of blisse they know.

Thou seest there's giuen so great might
To some that are but clay as I,
Their very anger can affright,
Which, if in any thou espie.
  Thus thinke; If Mortals frownes strike feare,
  How dreadfull will Gods wrath appeare?

By my late hopes that now are crost,
Consider those that firmer be:
And make the freedome I haue lost,
A meanes that may remember thee:

Had

The Shepheards Hunting.

Had Christ, *not thy Redeemer bin,*
What horrid thrall thou had'st been in.

These yron chaines, these bolts of steele,
Which other poore offenders grind,
The wants and cares which they doe feele,
May bring some greater thing to mind:
   For by their griefe thou shalt doe well,
   To thinke vpon the paines of Hell.

Or, when through me thou seest a Man
Condemn'd vnto a mortall death,
How sad he lookes, how pale, how wan,
Drawing with feare his panting breath:
   Thinke, if in that, such griefe thou see,
   How sad will, Goe yee cursed *be.*

Againe, when he that fear'd to Dye
(Past hope) doth see his Pardon brought,
Reade but the ioy that's in his eye,
And then conuey it to thy thought:
   There thinke, betwixt thy heart and thee,
   How sweet will, Come yee blessed, *bee.*

Thus if thou doe, though closed here,
My bondage I shall deeme the lesse,
I neither shall haue cause to feare,
Nor yet bewaile my sad distresse:

                                      For

The Shepheards Hunting.

For whether liue, or pine, or dye,
We shall haue blisse eternally.

Willy.

Trust me I see the *Cage* doth some *Birds* good,
And if they doe not suffer too much wrong,
Will teach them sweeter descants then the wood:
Beleeue't, I like the subiect of thy *Song*,
It shewes thou art in no distempred mood:
But cause to heare the residue I long,
  My Sheepe to morrow I will neerer bring,
  And spend the day to heare thee talk and sing.

Yet e're we part, *Philarete*, areed,
Of whom thou learnd'st to make such songs as these,
I neuer yet heard any Shepheards reede
Tune in mishap, a straine that more could please;
Surely, *Thou* do'st inuoke at this thy neede
Some power, that we neglect in other layes:
  For heer's a Name, and words, that but few swaines
  Haue mention'd at their meeting on the Plaines.

Philarete.

Indeed 'tis true; and they are sore to blame,
They doe so much neglect it in their Songs,
For, thence proceedeth such a worthy fame,
As is not subiect vnto Enuies wrongs:
That, is the most to be respected *name*
Of our true *Pan*, whose worth sits on all tongues:
                                                And

The Shepheards Hunting.

And what the ancient Shepheards vſe to prayſe
In ſacred *Anthemes*, vpon Holy-dayes.

Hee that firſt taught his Muſicke ſuch a ſtraine
Was that ſweet Shepheard, who (vntill a King)
Kept Sheepe vpon the hony-milky Plaine,
That is inrich't by *Iordans* watering;
He in his troubles eas'd the bodies paines,
By meaſures rais'd to the Soules rauiſhing:
  And his ſweet numbers onely moſt diuine,
  Gaue firſt the being to this Song of mine.

Willy.
Let his good ſpirit euer with thee dwell,
That I might heare ſuch Muſicke euery day.

Philarete.
Thankes, *Swaine:* but harke, thy *Weather* rings his Bell.
And *Swaines* to fold, or homeward driue away.

Willy.
And yon goes *Cuddy*, therefore fare thou well:
I'le make his Sheepe for mee a little ſtay;
And, if thou thinke it fit, I'le bring him to,
Next morning hither.———————————

Philarete.
——————————Prethee, *Willy*, do.

FINIS.

The Shepheards Hunting.

The second Eglogue.

THE ARGVMENT.
Cuddy *here relates, how all*
Pitty Philarete's *thrall.*
Who, requested, doth relate
The true cause of his estate;
Which broke off, because 'twas long,
They begin, a three-man-Song.

WILLY. CVDDY. PHILARETE.

Willy.
LO, *Philaret*, thy old friend heere, and I,
Are come to visit thee in these thy Bands,
Whil'st both our Flocks in an *Inclosure* by,
Doe picke the thin grasse from the fallowed lands.
He tels me thy restraint of liberty,
Each one throughout the Country vnderstands:
  And there is not a gentle-natur'd *Lad*
  On all these *Downes*, but for thy sake is sad.
  Cuddy.

The Shepheards Hunting.

Cuddy.
Not thy acquaintance, and thy friends alone,
Pitty thy clofe reftraint, as friends fhould doe:
But fome that haue but feene thee, for thee moane:
Yea, many that did neuer fee thee to.
Some deeme thee in a fault, and moft in none;
So diuers wayes doe diuers *Rumors* goe
   And at all meetings where our *Shepheards* bee,
   Now the maine Newes that's extant, is of thee.

Philarete.
Why, this is fomewhat yet: had I but kept
Sheepe on the *Mountaines*, till the day of doome,
My *name* fhould in obfcuritie haue flept
In *Brakes*, in *Briars, fhrubbed Furze* and *Broome*.
Into the Worlds wide eare it had not crept,
Nor in fo many mens thoughts found a roome:
   But what caufe of my fufferings doe they know?
   Good *Cuddy*, tell me, how doth *rumour* goe?

Cuddy.
Faith 'tis vncertaine; fome fpeake this, fome that:
Some dare fay nought, yet feeme to thinke a caufe,
And many a one prating he knowes not what;
Comes out with *Prouerbes* and *old ancient fawes*,
As if he thought thee guiltleffe, and yet not:
Then doth he fpeake halfe *Sentences*, then pawfe:
   That what the moft would fay, we may fuppofe;
   But, what to fay, the *Rumour* is, none knowes.
                                      Philarete.

The Shepheards Hunting.

Philarete.
Nor care I greatly ; for, it skils not much,
What the vnſteady common-people deemes,
His *Conſcience* doth not alwaies feele leaſt touch,
That blameleſſe in the ſight of others ſeemes :
My cauſe is honeſt, and becauſe 'tis ſuch,
I hold it ſo, and not for mens eſteemes :
   If they ſpeake iuſtly well of mee, I'me glad ;
   If falſely euill, it ne're makes me ſad.

Willy.
I like that mind : but, *Shepheard,* you are quite
Beſide the matter that I long to heare :
Remember what you promis'd yeſter-night,
Youl'd put vs off with other talke, I feare ;
Thou know'ſt that honeſt *Cuddies* heart's vpright,
And none but he, except my ſelfe, is neere :
   Come therefore, and betwixt vs two relate,
   The true occaſion of thy preſent ſtate.

Philarete.
My Friends I will ; You know I am a *Swaine,*
That kept a poore Flocke on a barren *Plaine* :
Who though it ſeemes, I could doe nothing leſſe,
Can make a *Song,* and woe a *Shepheardeſſe.*
And not alone the faireſt where I liue,
Haue heard me ſing, and fauours daign'd to giue :
But, though I ſay't, the *nobleſt Nymph* of *Thame,*
Hath grac'd my *Verſe,* vnto my greater fame.
                                         Yet,

The Shepheards Hunting.

Yet, being young, and not much feeking prayfe,
I was not noted out for *Shepheards layes* :
Nor feeding Flocks, as, you know, others be :
For the delight that moft poffeffed me
Was hunting *Foxes, Wolues*, and *Beafts* of *Prey :*
That fpoyle our *Foulds*, and beare our *Lambs* away.
For this, as alfo for the loue I beare
Vnto my *Country*, I laid-by all *care*
Of *gaine*, or of *preferment*, with *defire*
Onely to keepe that ftate I had entire.
And like a true growne *Huntfman* fought to fpeed
My felfe with *Hounds* of rare and choyfeft breed,
Whofe *Names* and *Natures* ere I further goe,
Becaufe you are my friends I'le let you know.
My firft efteemed Dogge that I did finde,
Was by *defcent* of olde *Acteons* kinde ;
A *Brache*, which if I doe not aime amiffe,
For all the world is iuft like one of his *:*
She's named *Loue*, and fcarce yet knowes her duty ;
Her Damme's my Ladies pretty *Beagle, Beauty.*
I bred her vp my felfe with wondrous charge,
Vntill fhe grew to be exceeding large,
And waxt fo wanton, that I did abhorre it,
And put her out amongft my neighbours for it.
The next is *Luft*, a Hound that's kept abroad
Mongft fome of mine acquaintance, but a Toad
Is not more loathfome : 'tis a Curre will range
Extreamely, and is euer full of mange :

           And

The Shepheards Hunting.

And caufe it is infectious, fhe's not wunt
To come among the reft, but when they hunt.
Hate is the third, a Hound both deepe and long :
His *Sire* is *True*, or elfe fuppofed *Wrong.*
He'le haue a fnap at all that paffe him by,
And yet purfues his game moft eagerly.
With him goes *Enuie* coupled, a leane Curre,
And yet fhe'le hold out, hunt we ne're fo farre :
She pineth much, and feedeth little to,
Yet ftands and fnarleth at the reft that doe.
Then there's *Reuenge*, a wondrous deep-mouth'd dog,
So fleet, I'me faine to hunt him with a clog,
Yet many times he'le much out-ftrip his bounds,
And hunts not clofely with the other Hounds :
He'le venter on a *Lyon* in his *ire* ;
Curft *Choller* was his *Damme*, and *Wrong* his *Sire.*
This *Choller*, is a *Brache*, that's very old,
And fpends her mouth too-much to haue it hold :
She's very teafty ; an vnpleafing Curre,
That bites the very Stones, if they but fturre :
Or when that ought but her difpleafure moues,
She'le bite and fnap at any one fhe loues.
But my quicke fcented'ft Dogge is *Iaeloufie*,
The trueft of this breede's in *Italie.*
The *Damme* of mine would hardly fill a Gloue,
It was a *Ladies* little Dogge, cal'd *Loue* :
The *Sire* a poore deformed Curre, nam'd *Feare* ;
As fhagged and as rough as is a *Beare :*
And

The Shepheards Hunting.

And yet the Whelpe turn'd after neither kinde,
For he is very large, and nere-hand blinde.
Farre-off, hee feemeth of a pretty culler,
But doth not proue fo, when you view him fuller.
A vile fufpitious Beaft; whofe lookes are bad,
And I doe feare in time he will grow mad.
To him I couple *Auarice*, ftill poore;
Yet fhee deuoures as much as twenty more:
A thoufand Horfe fhee in her paunch can put,
Yet whine, as if fhe had an emptie gut;
And hauing gorg'd what might a Land haue found,
Shee'le catch for more, and, hide it in the ground.
Ambition is a Hound as greedy full;
But hee for all the daintieft bits doth cull:
Hee fcornes to licke vp Crumbs beneath the Table,
Hee'le fetch't from boards and fhelues, if he be able:
Nay, hee can climbe, if neede be; and for that
With him I hunt the *Martine*, and the *Cat*:
And yet fometimes in mounting, hee's fo quicke,
Hee fetches falls, are like to breake his necke.
Feare is wel-mouth'd, but fubiect to *Diftruft*;
A Stranger cannot make him take a Cruft:
A little thing will foone his courage quaile,
And 'twixt his legges hee euer claps his Taile.
With him, *Defpaire*, now, often coupled goes,
Which by his roring mouth each *hunts-man* knowes.
None hath a better minde vnto the game;
But hee giues off, and alwaies feemeth lame.

My

The Shepheards Hunting.

My bloud-hound *Cruelty*, as fwift as wind,
Hunts to the death, and neuer comes behind ;
Who, but fhe's ftrapt, and mufled to, withall,
Would eate her fellowes and the prey and all.
And yet, fhe cares not much for any food ;
Vnleffe it be the pureft harmeleffe blood.
   All thefe are kept abroad at charge of meny,
They doe not coft me in a yeare a penny.
But there's two couple of a midling fize,
That feldome paffe the fight of my owne eyes.
Hope, on whofe head I'ue laid my life to pawne ;
Compaffion, that on euery one will fawne.
This would, when 'twas a whelpe, with *Rabets* play
Or *Lambes*, and let them goe vnhurt away :
Nay, now fhe is of growth, fhee'le now and then
Catch you a *Hare*, and let her goe agen.
The two laft, *Ioy*, and *Sorrow* ; make me wonder,
For they can ne're agree, nor bide afunder.
Ioy's euer wanton, and no order knowes,
She'le run at *Larkes*, or ftand and barke at *Crowes*.
Sorrow goes by her, and ne're moues his eye :
Yet both doe ferue to helpe make vp the cry :
Then comes behinde all thefe to beare the bafe,
Two couple more of a farre larger Race,
Such wide-mouth'd *Trollops*, that 'twould doe you good,
To heare their loud-loud *Ecchoes* teare the Wood :
There's *Vanity*, who by her gaudy *Hide*,
May farre away from all the reft be fpide,
          K k   Though

The Shepheards Hunting.

Though huge, yet quicke, for she's now here, now there;
Nay, looke about you, and she's euery where:
Yet euer with the rest, and still in chace,
Right so, *Inconstancie* fils euery place;
And yet so strange a fickle natur'd Hound,
Looke for her, and she's no where to be found.
Weakenesse is no faire Dogge vnto the eye,
And yet she hath her proper qualitie.
But there's *Presumption*, when he heat hath got,
He drownes the *Thunder*, and the *Cannon-shot*:
And when at Start, he his full roaring makes,
The Earth doth tremble, and the Heauen shakes:
These were my Dogs, ten couple iust in all,
Whom by the name of *Satyres* I doe call:
Mad Curs they be, and I can ne're come nigh them,
But I'me in danger to be bitten by them.
Much paines I tooke, and spent dayes not a few,
To make them keepe together, and hunt true:
Which yet I doe suppose had neuer bin,
But that I had a *Scourge* to keepe them in.
Now when that I this Kennell first had got,
Out of mine owne Demeanes I hunted not,
Saue on these Downes, or among yonder *Rocks*,
After those beasts that spoyl'd our Parish Flockes:
Nor during that time, was I euer wont,
With all my Kennell in one day to hunt:
Nor had done yet, but that this other yeere,
Some Beasts of *Prey* that haunt the *Deserts* heere,
                                                        Did

The Shepheards Hunting.

Did not alone for many *Nights* together
Deuoure, fometime a *Lambe*, fometime a *Weather*:
And fo difquiet many a poore mans Heard,
But thereof loofing all were much afeard.
Yea, I among the reft, did fare as bad,
Or rather worfe; for the beft *Ewes I had,   **Hopes.*
(Whofe breed fhould be my meanes of life and gaine,
Were in one Euening by thefe *Monfters* flaine:
Which mifchiefe I refolued to repay,
Or elfe grow defperate and hunt all away.
For in a furie fuch as you fhall fee
Hunts-men, in miffing of their fport will be)
I vow'd a *Monfter* fhould not lurke about
In all this *Prouince*, but I'de finde him out.
And thereupon without refpect or *care*,
How *lame*, how *full*, or how *vnfit* they were,
In haft vnkennell'd all my roaring crew,
Who were as mad, as if my mind they knew;
And e're they trail'd a flight-fhot, the fierce Curres,
Had rous'd a *Hart*, and through *Brakes*, *Bryars*, and *Furres*
Follow'd at gaze fo clofe, that *Loue* and *Feare*
Got in together, and had furely, there
Quite ouerthrowne him, but that *Hope* thruft in
'Twixt both, and fau'd the pinching of his skin.
Whereby he fcap't, till courfing ouerthwart,
Defpaire came in, and grip't him to the hart.
I hallowed in the refdue to the fall,
And for an entrance, there I flefh't them all:

The Shepheards Hunting.

Which hauing done, I dip'd my ftaffe in blood
And onward led my *Thunder* to the Wood;
Where what they did, I'le tell you out anon,
My keeper calles me, and I muft be gon.
Goe, if you pleafe a while, attend your Flocks,
And when the *Sunne* is ouer yonder Rocks,
Come to this *Caue* againe, where I will be,
If that my *Gardian*, fo much fauour me.
   Yet if you pleafe, let vs three fing a ftraine,
   Before you turne your fheepe into the Plaine.

Willie.
I am content.─────────

Cuddy.
─────────As well content am I.

Philarete.
Then *Will* begin, and wee'le the reft fupply.

Song.

Willie.
SHepheard, would thefe Gates were ope,
Thou might'ft take with vs thy fortunes.
Phil.

The Shepheards Hunting.

Philarete.

No, I'le make this narrow scope,
(Since my Fate doth so importune)
  Meanes vnto a wider Hope.

Cuddy.

Would thy Shepheardesse were here,
  Who belou'd, loues so dearely?

Philarete.

Not for both your Flocks, I sweare,
And the gaine they yeeld you yeerely,
  Would I so much wrong my Deare.

Yet, to me, nor to this Place,
Would she now be long a stranger:
She would hold it in disgrace,
(If she fear'd not more my danger)
  Where I am to shew her face.

Willie.

Shepheard, we would wish no harmes,
But something that might content thee.

Philarete.

Wish me then within her armes;
And that wish will ne're repent me,
  If your wishes might proue charmes.

Willie.

The Shepheards Hunting.

Willie.

Be thy Prison her embrace,
Be thy ayre her sweetest breathing.

Cuddy.

Be thy prospect her sweet Face,
For each looke a kisse bequeathing,
  And appoint thy selfe the place.

Philarete.

Nay pray, hold there, for I should scantly then,
Come meete you here this afternoone agen:
But fare you well, since wishes haue no power,
Let vs depart and keepe the pointed houre.

The

The Shepheards Hunting.

The third Eglogue.

> THE ARGVMENT.
> Philarete *with his three Friends,*
> *Heare his hunting storie ends.*
> *Kinde* Alexis *with much ruth,*
> *Wailes the banish't Shepheards youth*:
> *But he slighteth Fortunes slings,*
> *And in spight of Thraldome sings.*

PHILARETE. CVDDY. ALEXIS. WILLY.

Philarete.

SO, now I fee y'are *Shepheards* of your word,
Thus were you wont to promife, and to doe.

Cuddy.

More then our promife is, we can afford,
We come our felues, and bring another to:
Alexis, whom thou know'ft well is no foe:

The Shepheards Hunting.

Who loues thee much: and I doe know that he
Would faine a hearer of thy Hunting be.

Philarete.

Alexis you are welcome, for you know
You cannot be but welcome where I am;
You euer were a friend of mine in ſhow,
And I haue found you are indeed the ſame:
Vpon my firſt reſtraint you hither came,
   And proffered me more tokens of your loue,
   Then it were fit my ſmall deſerts ſhould proue.

Alexis.

'Tis ſtill your vſe to vnderpriſe your merit;
Be not ſo coy to take my proffered loue,
'Twill neither vnbeſeeme your *worth* nor *ſpirit*.
To offer court'ſie doth thy friend behoue:
And which are ſo, this is a place to proue.
   Then once againe I ſay, if *cauſe* there be.
   Firſt make a *tryall*, if thou pleaſe, of me.

Philarete.

Thankes good *Alexis*; ſit downe by me heere,
I haue a taske, theſe *Shepheards* know, to doe;
A *Tale* already told this Morne well neere,
With which I very faine would forward goe,
And am as willing thou ſhould'ſt heare it to:
   But thou canſt neuer vnderſtand this laſt,
   Till I haue alſo told thee what is paſt.

Willie.

The Shepheards Hunting.

Willy.

It shall not neede, for I so much presum'd,
I on your mutuall friendships, might be bold,
That I a freedome to my selfe assum'd,
To make him know, what is already told.
If I haue done amisse, then you may scold.
   But in my telling I preuised this,
   He knew not whose, nor to what end it is.

Philarete.

Well, now he may, for heere my Tale goes on:
My eager Dogges and I to Wood are gon.
Where, beating through the *Conuerts*, euery Hound
A seuerall *Game* had in a moment found:
I rated them, but they pursu'd their pray,
And as it fell (by hap) tooke all one way.
Then I began with quicker speed to follow,
And teaz'd them on, with a more chearefull hallow:
That soone we passed many weary miles,
Tracing the subtile game through all their wiles.
These doubl'd, those re-doubled on the scent,
Still keeping in full chase where ere they went.
Vp *Hils*, downe *Cliffes*, through *Bogs*, and ouer *Plaines*,
Stretching their *Musicke* to the highest straines.
That when some Thicket hid them from mine eye,
My eare was rauish'd with their melodie.
Nor crost we onely Ditches, Hedges, Furrowes,
But Hamlets, Tithings, Parishes, and Burrowes:
                              They

The Shepheards Hunting.

They followed where fo eu'r the game did go,
Through Kitchin, Parlor, Hall, and Chamber to.
And, as they paff'd the *City*, and the *Court*,
My *Prince* look'd out, and daign'd to view my fport.
Which then (although I fuffer for it now)
(If fome fay true) he liking did allow;
And fo much (had I had but wit to ftay)
I might my felfe (perhaps) haue heard him fay.
But I, that time, as much as any daring,
More for my pleafure then my fafetie caring;
Seeing frefh game from euery couert rife,
(Croffing by thoufands ftill before their eyes)
Rufh'd in, and then following clofe my *Hounds*,
Some beafts I found lie dead, fome full of wounds,
Among the willows, fcarce with ftrength to moue,
One I found heere, another there, whom *Loue*
Had grip'd to death: and, in the felfe-fame ftate,
Lay one deuour'd by *Enuy*, one by *Hate*;
Luft had bit fome, but I foone paft befide them,
Their feftr'd wounds fo ftuncke, none could abide them.
Choller hurt diuers, but *Reuenge* kild more:
Feare frighted all, behinde him and before.
Defpaire draue on a huge and mighty heape,
Forcing fome downe from *Rocks* and *Hils* to leape:
Some into water, fome into the fire,
So on themfelues he made them wreake his *ire*.
But I remember, as I paff'd that way,
Where the great *King* and *Prince* of *Shepheards* lay,
                                                About

The Shepheards Hunting.

About the wals were hid, fome (once more knowne)
That my fell Curre *Ambition* had o'rethrowne:
Many I heard, purfu'd by *Pitty*, cry;
And oft I faw my *Bloud-Hound, Cruelty*,
Eating her paffage euen to the hart,
Whither once gotten, fhe is loath to part.
All pli'd it well, and made fo loud a cry,
'Twas heard beyond the Shores of *Britany*.
Some rated them, fome ftorm'd, fome lik'd the *game*,
Some thought *me worthy praife*, fome *worthy blame*.
But I, not fearing th'one, mif-fteeming t'other,
Both, in fhrill hallowes and loud yernings fmother.
Yea, the ftrong mettled, and my long-breath'd crew,
Seeing the *game* increafing in their view,
Grew the more frolicke, and the courfes length
Gaue better breath, and added to their ftrength.
Which *Ioue* perceiuing, for *Ioue* heard their cries
Rumbling amongft the *Spheares concauities:*
Hee mark'd their *courfe*, and *courages* increafe,
Saying, 'twere pitty fuch a chafe fhould ceafe.
And therewith fwore their mouthes fhould neuer waft,
But hunt as long's mortality did laft.
Soone did they feele the power of his great gift,
And I began to finde their pace more fwift:
I follow'd, and I rated, but in vaine
Striu'd to o'retake, or take them vp againe.
They neuer ftayed fince, nor nights nor dayes,
But to and fro ftill run a thoufand wayes:
          Yea,

The Shepheards Hunting.

Yea, often to this place where now I lie,
They'l wheele about to cheare me with their cry;
And one day in good time will vengeance take
On some offenders, for their Masters sake:
For know, my Friends, my freedome in this sort
For them I lose, and making my selfe sport.

Willy.
Why? was there any harme at all in this?

Philarete.
No, *Willy*, and I hope yet none there is.

Willy.
How comes it then?————————

Philarete.
—————————Note, and I'le tell the how?
Thou know'st that *Truth* and *Innocency* now,
If plac'd with meannesse, suffers more despight
Then *Villainies*, accompan'ed with might.
But thus it fell, while that my *Hounds* pursu'd
Their noysome prey, and euery field laid strew'd
With *Monsters*, hurt and slaine; vpon a beast,
More subtile, and more noysome then the rest,
My leane-flanckt Bitch, cald *Enuy*, hapt to light:
And, as her wont is, did so surely bite,
That, though shee left behinde small outward smart,
The wounds were deepe, and rankled to the hart.
This, joyning to some other, that of late,
Were very eagerly pursu'd by *Hate*,

(To

The Shepheards Hunting.

(To fit their purpofe hauing taken leafure)
Did thus confpire to worke me a difpleafure.
For imitation, farre furpaffing *Apes*,
They laide afide their *Foxe* and *Woluifh fhapes*,
And fhrowded in the skinnes of harmleffe Sheepe
Into by-wayes, and open paths did creepe;
Where, they (as hardly drawing breath) did ly,
Shewing their wounds to euery paffer by;
To make them thinke that they were fheepe fo foyl'd,
And by my Dogges, in their late hunting, fpoyl'd.
Befide, fome other that enuy'd my game,
And, for their paftime, kept fuch *Monfters* tame:
As, you doe know, there's many for their pleafure
Keepe Foxes, Beares, & Wolues, as fome great treafure:
Yea, many get their liuing by them to,
And fo did ftore of thefe, I fpeake of, do.
Who, feeing that my *Kennell* had affrighted,
Or hurt fome *Vermine* wherein they delighted;
And finding their owne power by much to weake,
Their *Malice* on my *Innocence* to wreake,
Swolne with the deepeft rancour of defpight,
Some of our greateft *Shepheards* Folds by night
They clofely entred; and there hauing ftain'd
Their hands in *villany*, of mee they plain'd,
Affirming, (without *fhame*, or *honefty*,)
I, and my Dogges, had done it purpofely.
Whereat they ftorm'd, and cald mee to a *tryall*,
Where *Innocence* preuailes not, nor *denyall*:
                                                    But

The Shepheards Hunting.

But for that *caufe*, heere in this place I lie,
Where none fo merry as my dogges, and I.

Cuddy.

Beleeue it, heere's a *Tale* will futen well,
For *Shepheards* in another *Age* to tell.

Willy.

And thou fhalt be remembred with delight,
By this, hereafter, many a *Winters night.*
For, of this fport another *Age* will ring;
Yea, *Nymphes* that are vnborne thereof fhall fing,
  And not a *Beauty* on our Greenes fhall play,
  That hath not heard of this thy hunting day.

Philarete.

It may be fo, for if that gentle *Swaine*,
Who wonnes by *Tauy*, on the *Wefterne plaine*,
Would make the *Song*, fuch life his *Verfe* can giue,
Then I doe know my *Name* might euer liue.

Alexis.

But tell me; are our *Plaines* and *Nymphs* forgot,
And canft thou frolicke in thy trouble be?

Philarete.

Can I, *Alexis*, fayft thou? Can I not,
That am refolu'd to fcorne more mifery?

                                      Alexis.

The Shepheards Hunting.

Alexis.

Oh, but that youth's yet greene, and young bloud hot,
And *liberty* muſt needs be ſweet to thee.
But, now moſt ſweet whil'ſt euery buſhy *Vale,*
And *Groue,* and *Hill,* rings of the *Nightingale.*

Me thinkes, when thou remembreſt thoſe *ſweet layes*
Which thou would'ſt leade thy *Shepheardeſſe* to heare,
Each Euening tyde among the *Leauy ſprayes,*
The thought of that ſhould make thy freedome deare :
For now, whil'ſt euery *Nymph* on *Holy-dayes*
Sports with ſome *iolly Lad,* and maketh cheere,
   Thine, ſighes for thee, and mew'd vp from reſort,
   Will neither play her ſelfe, nor ſee their ſport.

Thoſe *Shepheards* that were many a Morning wont,
Vnto their Boyes to leaue the tender *Heard* ;
And beare thee company when thou didſt hunt ;
Me thinkes the ſport thou haſt ſo gladly ſhar'd
Among thoſe *Swaynes* ſhould make thee thinke vpon't,
For't ſeemes all vaine, now, that was once indear'd.
   It cannot be : ſince I could make relation,
   How for leſſe *cauſe* thou haſt beene deepe in *paſſion.*

Philarete.

'Tis true : my tender heart was euer yet
Too capable of ſuch conceits as theſe ;
I neuer ſaw that *Obiect,* but from it,
The *Paſſions* of my *Loue* I could encreaſe.
                                          Thoſe

The Shepheards Hunting.

Those things which moue not other men a whit,
I can, and doe make vse of, if I please:
   When I am sad, to sadnesse I apply,
   Each *Bird*, and *Tree*, and *Flowre* that I passe by.

So, when I will be merry, I aswell
Something for mirth from euery thing can draw,
From *Miserie*, from *Prisons*, nay from *Hell*:
And as when to my *minde*, *griefe* giues a flaw,
Best comforts doe but make my woes more fell:
So when I'me bent to *Mirth*, from mischiefes paw.
   (Though ceas'd vpon me) I would something cull,
   That spight of *care*, should make my *ioyes* more full.

I feele those wants, *Alexis*, thou doest name,
Which spight of youths affections I sustaine;
Or else, for what is't I haue gotten *Fame*,
And am more knowne then many an *elder Swaine*?
If such desires I had not learn'd to tame,
(Since many pipe much better on this *Plaine*:)
   But tune your *Reedes*, and I will in a *Song*,
   Expresse my *Care*, and how I take this *Wrong*.

Sonnet.

I That ere'st-while the worlds sweet Ayre did draw,
 (Grac'd by the fairest euer Mortall saw;)
                                                    Now

The Shepheards Hunting.

Now closely pent, with walles of Ruth-lesse stone,
Consume my Dayes, and Nights and all alone.

When I was wont to sing of Shepheards loues,
My walkes were Fields, and Downes, and Hils, and Groues:
But now (alas) so strict is my hard doome,
Fields, Downes, Hils, Groues, and al's but one poore roome.

Each Morne, as soone as Day-light did appeare,
With Natures Musicke Birds would charme mine eare:
Which now (instead) of their melodious straines,
Heare, ratling Shackles, Gyues, and Boults, and Chaines.

But, though that all the world's delight forsake me,
I haue a Muse, *and she shall Musicke make me:*
Whose ayrie Notes, in spight of closest cages,
Shall giue content to me, and after ages.

Nor doe I passe for all this outward ill,
My hearts the same, and vndeiected still;
And which is more then some in freedome winne,
I haue true rest, and peace, and ioy within.

And then my Mind, that spight of prison's free,
When ere she pleases any where can be;
Shee's in an houre, in France, Rome, Turky, Spaine,
In Earth, in Hell, in Heauen, and here againe.

The Shepheards Hunting.

Yet there's another comfort in my woe,
My caufe is fpread, and all the world may know,
My fault's no more, but fpeaking Truth, and Reafon;
No Debt, nor Theft, nor Murther, Rape, or Treafon.

Nor fhall my foes with all their Might and Power,
Wipe out their fhame, nor yet this fame of our:
Which when they finde, they fhall my fate enuie,
Till they grow leane, and ficke, and mad, and die.

Then though my Body here in Prifon rot,
And my wrong'd Satyres feeme a while forgot:
Yet, when both Fame, and life hath left thofe men,
My Verfe and I'le reuiue, and liue agen.

So thus enclos'd, I beare afflictions load,
But with more true content then fome abroad;
For whilft their thoughts, doe feele my Scourges fting,
In bands I'le leape, and dance, and laugh, and fing.

Alexis.

Why now I fee thou droup'ft not with thy care,
Neither exclaim'ft thou on thy hunting day;
But doft with vnchang'd refolution beare,
The heauy burthen of exile away.
All that did truely know thee, did conceaue,
Thy actions with thy fpirit ftill agree'd;
Their good conceit thou doeft no whit bereaue,
But fheweft that thou art ftill thy felfe indeed.

If

The Shepheards Hunting.

If that thy mind to bafeneffe now defcends,
Thou'lt iniure *Vertue*, and deceiue thy friends.

Willie.

Alexis, he will iniure *Vertue* much,
But more his friends, and moſt of all himſelfe,
If on that common barre his minde but touch,
It wrackes his fame vpon difgraces fhelfe.
Whereas if thou ſteere on that happy courſe,
Which in thy iuſt aduenture is begun ;
No thwarting Tide, nor aduerſe blaſt ſhall force
Thy *Barke* without the *Channels* bounds to run.
Thou art the ſame thou wert, for ought I ſee,
When thou didſt freely on the Mountaines hunt,
In nothing changed yet, vnleſſe it be
More merrily difpos'd then thou wert wont.
Still keepe thee thus, ſo other ſhall know,
Vertue can giue content in midſt of woe.
And ſhe (though *mightines* with frownes doth threat)
That, to be *Innocent*, is to be *great*,
Thriue and farewell.————

Alexis.
—————In this thy trouble flouriſh.

Cuddy.
While thoſe that wiſh thee ill, fret, pine, and periſh.

The Shepheards Hunting.

The fourth Eglogue.

> **THE ARGVMENT.**
> Philaret *on* Willy *calls*,
> *To sing out his Pastorals:*
> *Warrants* Fame *shall grace his Rimes,*
> *Spight of* Enuy *and the Times*;
> *And shewes how in care he vses,*
> *To take comfort from his Muses.*

PHILARETE. WILLIE.

Philarete.

PRethee, *Willy* tell me this,
What new accident there is,
That thou (once the blytheſt Lad)
Art become ſo wondrous ſad?
And ſo careleſſe of thy quill,
As if thou had'ſt loſt thy skill?
Thou wert wont to charme thy flocks,
And among the maſſy rocks

Haſt

The Shepheards Hunting.

Haft fo chear'd me with thy Song,
That I haue forgot my wrong.
Something hath thee furely croft,
That thy old want thou haft loft.
Tell me: Haue I ought mif-faid
That hath made thee ill-apaid?
Hath fome Churle done thee a fpight?
Doft thou miffe a Lambe to night?
Frowns thy faireft *Shepheards* Laffe?
Or how comes this ill to paffe?
Is there any difcontent
Worfe then this my banifhment?

       Willie.

Why, doth that fo euill feeme
That thou nothing worft doft deeme?
Shepheards, there full many be,
That will change *Contents* with thee.
Thofe that choofe their Walkes at will,
On the Valley or the Hill.
Or thofe pleafures boaft of can,
Groues or Fields may yeeld to man:
Neuer come to know the reft,
Wherewithall thy minde is bleft.
Many a one that oft reforts
To make vp the troope at fports.
And in company fome while,
Happens to ftraine forth a fmile.

The Shepheards Hunting.

Feeles more want, and outward ſmart,
And more inward griefe of hart
Then this place can bring to thee,
While thy mind remaineth free.
Thou bewail'ſt my want of mirth,
But what find'ſt thou in this earth,
Wherein ought may be beleeu'd
Worth to make me Ioy'd ; or grieu'd ?
And yet feele I *(*naitheleſſe*)*
Part of both I muſt confeſſe.
Sometime, I of mirth doe borrow,
Otherwhile as much of ſorrow ;
But, my preſent ſtate is ſuch,
As, nor Ioy, nor grieue I much.

Philarete.

Why, hath *Willy* then ſo long
Thus forborne his wonted Song ?
Wherefore doth he now let fall,
His well-tuned *Paſtorall?*
And my eares that muſike barre,
Which I more long after farre,
Then the liberty I want.

Willy.

That, were very much to grant,
But, doth this hold alway lad,
Thoſe that ſing not, muſt be ſad ?

Did'ſt

The Shepheards Hunting.

Did'ſt thou euer that Bird heare
Sing well; that ſings all the yeare?
Tom the *Piper* doth not play
Till he weares his Pipe away:
There's a time to ſlacke the ſtring,
And a time to leaue to ſing.

Philarete.

Yea; but no man now is ſtill,
That can ſing, or tune a quill.
Now to chant it, were but reaſon;
Song and *Muſicke* are in ſeaſon.
Now in this ſweet iolly tide,
Is the earth in all her pride:
The faire Lady of the *May*
Trim'd vp in her beſt array;
Hath inuited all the Swaines,
With the Laſſes of the Plaines.
To attend vpon her ſport
At the places of reſort.
Coridon (with his bould Rout)
Hath alredy been about
For the elder Shepheards dole,
And fetch'd in the *Summer-Pole*:
Whil'ſt the reſt haue built a *Bower*,
To defend them from a ſhower;
Seil'd ſo cloſe, with boughes all greene,
Tytan cannot pry betweene.

The Shepheards Hunting.

Now the *Dayrie-Wenches* dreame
Of their Strawberries and Creame:
And each doth her felfe aduance
To be taken in, to dance:
Euery one that knowes to fing,
Fits him for his Carrolling:
So do thofe that hope for meede,
Either by the Pipe or Reede:
And though I am kept away,
I doe heare (this very day)
Many learned Groomes doe wend,
For the Garlands to contend.
Which a Nimph that hight *Defart,*
(Long a ftranger in this part).
With her own faire hand hath wrought
A rare worke (they fay) paft thought,
As appeareth by the name,
For fhe cals them *Wreathes of Fame.*
She hath fet in their due place
Eu'ry flowre that may grace;
And among a thoufand moe,
(Whereof fome but ferue for fhew)
She hath woue in *Daphnes* tree,
That they may not blafted be.
Which with *Time* fhe edg'd about,
Leaft the worke fhould rauell out.
And that it might wither neuer,
I intermixt it with *Liue-euer*.

Thefe

The Shepheards Hunting.

These are to be shar'd among,
Those that doe excell for song:
Or their passions can rehearse
In the smooth'st and sweetest verse.
Then, for those among the rest,
That can play and pipe the best.
There's a Kidling with the Damme,
A fat Weather, and a Lambe.
And for those that leapen far,
Wrastle, Runne, and throw the Barre,
There's appointed guerdons to.
He, that best, the first can doe,
Shall, for his reward, be paid,
With a *Sheep-hooke*, faire in-laid
With fine Bone, of a strange Beast
That men bring out of the West.
For the next, a *Scrip* of red,
Tassel'd with fine coloured Thred,
There's prepared for their meed,
That in running make most speede,
(Or the cunning Measures foote)
Cups of turned *Maple-roote:*
Whereupon the skilfull man
Hath ingrau'd the *Loues* of *Pan*:
And the last hath for his due,
A fine Napkin wrought with blew.
Then, my *Willy*, why art thou
Carelesse of thy merit now?

What

The Shepheards Hunting.

What doſt thou heere, with a wight
That is ſhut vp from delight,
In a ſolitary den,
As not fit to liue with men?
Goe, my *Willy*, get thee gone,
Leaue mee in exile alone.
Hye thee to that merry throng,
And amaze them with thy *Song*.
Thou art young, yet ſuch a *Lay*
Neuer grac'd the month of May,
As (if they prouoke thy skill)
Thou canſt fit vnto thy *Quill*,
I with wonder heard thee ſing,
At our laſt yeeres Reuelling.
Then I with the reſt was free,
When vnknowne I noted thee:
And perceiu'd the ruder Swaines,
Enuy thy farre ſweeter ſtraines.
Yea, I ſaw the *Laſſes* cling
Round about thee in a Ring:
As if each one iealous were,
Any but her ſelfe ſhould heare.
And I know they yet do long
For the res'due of thy ſong.
Haſt thee then to ſing it forth;
Take the benefit of worth.
And *Deſert* will ſure bequeath
Fames faire Garland for thy wreath,
Hye thee, *Willy*, hye away.   *Willy*.

The Shepheards Hunting.

Willy.
Phila, rather let mee ſtay,
And be deſolate with thee,
Then at thoſe their *Reuels* bee,
Nought ſuch is my skill I wis,
As indeed thou deem'ſt it is.
But what ere it be, I muſt
Be content, and ſhall I truſt.
For a Song I doe not paſſe,
Mong'ſt my friends, but what (alas)
Should I haue to doe with them
That my Muſicke doe contemne?
Some there are, as well I wot,
That the ſame yet fauour not:
Yet I cannot well auow,
They my Carrols diſalow:
But ſuch malice I haue ſpid,
'Tis as much as if they did.

Philarete.
Willy, What may thoſe men be,
Are ſo ill, to malice thee?

Willy.
Some are worthy-well eſteem'd,
Some without worth are ſo deem'd.
Others of ſo baſe a ſpirit,
They haue nor eſteeme, nor merit.
                                        Phil.

The Shepheards Hunting.

Philarete.
What's the wrong?————

Willy.
————————A flight offence,
Wherewithall I can difpence;
But hereafter for their fake.
To my felfe I'le muficke make.

Philarete.
What, becaufe fome Clowne offends,
Wilt thou punifh all thy friends?

Willy.
Do not, *Phill*, mif-vnderftand mee,
Thofe that loue mee may command mee,
But, thou know'ft, I am but yong,
And the *Paftorall* I fung,
Is by fome fuppos'd to be,
(By a ftraine) too high for me:
So they kindly let me gaine,
Not my labour for my paine.
Truft me, I doe wonder why
They fhould me my owne deny.
Though I'me young, I fcorne to flit
On the wings of borrowed wit.
I'le make my owne feathers reare me,
Whither others cannot beare me.
                              Yet

The Shepheards Hunting.

Yet I'le keepe my skill in ſtore,
Till I'ue ſeene ſome Winters more.

Pillarete.

But, in earneſt, mean'ſt thou ſo?
Then thou art not wiſe, I trow:
Better ſhall aduiſe thee *Pan*,
For thou doſt not rightly than:
That's the ready way to blot
All the credit thou haſt got.
Rather in thy Ages prime,
Get another ſtart of Time:
And make thoſe that ſo fond be,
(Spight of their owne dulneſſe) ſee,
That the ſacred *Muſes* can
Make a childe in yeeres, a man.
It is knowne what thou canſt doe,
For it is not long agoe,
When that *Cuddy*, *Thou*, and *I*,
Each the others skill to try,
At Saint *Dunſtanes* charmed well,
(As ſome preſent there can tell)
Sang vpon a ſudden Theame,
Sitting by the Crimſon ſtreame.
Where, if thou didſt well or no,
Yet remaines the Song to ſhow,
Much experience more I'ue had,
Of thy skill (thou happy Lad)

And

The Shepheards Hunting.

And would make the world to know it;
But that time will further fhow it.
Enuy makes their tongues now runne
More then doubt of what is done.
For that needs muft be thy owne,
Or to be fome others knowne:
But how then wil't fuit vnto
What thou fhalt hereafter do?
Or I wonder where is hee,
Would with that fong part to thee.
Nay, were there fo mad a Swaine,
Could fuch glory fell for gaine;
Phœbus would not haue combin'd,
That gift with fo bafe a minde,
Neuer did the *Nine* impart
The fweet fecrets of their Art,
Vnto any that did fcorne,
We fhould fee their fauours worne.
Therefore vnto thofe that fay,
Where they pleas'd to fing a Lay,
They could doo't, and will not tho;
This I fpeake, for this I know:
None ere drunke the *Thefpian fpring*,
And knew how, but he did fing.
For, that once infus'd in man,
Makes him fhew't doe what he can.
Nay, thofe that doe onely fip,
Or, but eu'n their fingers dip
In

The Shepheards Hunting.

In that ſacred *Fount* (poore Elues)
Of that brood will ſhew themſelues.
Yea, in hope to get them fame,
They will ſpeake, though to their ſhame.
Let thoſe then at thee repine,
That by their wits meaſure thine ;
Needs thoſe Songs muſt be thine owne,
And that one day will be knowne.
That poore imputation to,
I my ſelfe do vndergoe :
But it will appeare ere long,
That 'twas Enuy ſought our wrong.
Who at twice-ten haue ſung more,
Then ſome will doe, at foureſcore.
Cheere thee (honeſt *Willy*) then,
And begin thy Song agen.

Willy.

Faine I would, but I doe feare
When againe my Lines they heare,
If they yeeld they are my Rimes,
They will faine ſome other Crimes ;
And 'tis no ſafe ventring-by
Where we ſee *Detraction* ly.
For doe what I can, I doubt,
She will picke ſome quarrell out ;
And I oft haue heard defended,
Little ſaid, is ſoone amended.

Phil.

The Shepheards Hunting.

Philarete.

See'ft thou not in cleareft dayes,
Oft thicke fogs cloud Heau'ns rayes.
And that vapours which doe breath
From the earths groffe wombe beneath,
Seeme not to vs with black fteames,
To pollute the Sunnes bright beames,
And yet vanifh into ayre,
Leauing it (vnblemifht) faire?
So (my *Willy*) fhall it bee
With *Detractions* breath on thee.
It fhall neuer rife fo hie,
As to ftaine thy Poefie.
As that Sunne doth oft exhale
Vapours from each rotten Vale;
Poefie fo fometime draines,
Groffe conceits from muddy braines;
Mifts of Enuy, fogs of fpight,
Twixt mens judgements and her light:
But fo much her power may do,
That fhee can diffolue them to.
If thy Verfe doe brauely tower,
As fhee makes wing, fhe gets power:
Yet the higher fhe doth fore,
Shee's affronted ftill the more:
Till fhee to the high'ft hath paft,
Then fhe refts with fame at laft,

        Let

The Shepheards Hunting.

Let nought therefore, thee affright:
But make forward in thy flight:
For if I could match thy Rime,
To the very Starres I'de clime.
There begin again, and flye,
Till I reach'd Æternity.
But (alaffe) my Mufe is flow:
For thy place fhee flags too low:
Yea, the more's her hapleffe fate,
Her fhort wings were clipt of late.
And poore I, her fortune ruing,
Am my felfe put vp a muing.
But if I my Cage can rid,
I'le flye where I neuer did.
And though for her fake I'me croft,
Though my beft hopes I haue loft,
And knew fhe would make my trouble
Ten times more then ten times double:
I fhould loue and keepe her to,
Spight of all the world could doe.
For though banifh't from my flockes,
And confin'd within thefe rockes,
Here I wafte away the light,
And confume the fullen Night,
She doth for my comfort ftay,
And keepes many cares away.
Though I miffe the flowry Fields,
With thofe fweets the Spring-tyde yeelds,

The Shepheards Hunting.

Though I may not fee thofe Groues,
Where the Shepheards chant their Loues,
(And the Laffes more excell,
Then the fweet voyc'd *Philomel*)
Though of all thofe pleafures paft,
Nothing now remaines at laft,
But *Remembrance* (poore reliefe)
That more makes, then mends my griefe :
Shee's my mindes companion ftill,
Maugre Enuies euill will.
(Whence fhe fhould be driuen to,
Wer't in mortals power to do.)
She doth tell me where to borrow
Comfort in the midft of forrow ;
Makes the defolateft place
To her prefence be a grace ;
And the blackeft difcontents
To be pleafing ornaments.
In my former dayes of bliffe,
Her diuine skill taught me this,
That from euery thing I faw,
I could fome inuention draw :
And raife pleafure to her height,
Through the meaneft obiects fight.
By the murmure of a fpring,
Or the leaft boughes rufteling.
By a Dazie whofe leaues fpred,
Shut when *Tytan* goes to bed ;

                                              Or

The Shepheards Hunting.

Or a fhady bufh or tree,
She could more infufe in mee,
Then all Natures beauties can,
In fome other wifer man.
By her helpe I alfo now,
Make this churlifh place allow
Some things that may fweeten gladnes,
In the very gall of fadnes.
The dull loanneffe, the blacke fhade,
That thefe hanging vaults haue made,
The ftrange Muficke of the waues,
Beating on thefe hollow Caues,
This blacke Den which Rocks emboffe
Ouer-growne with eldeft Moffe.
The rude Portals that giue light,
More to *Terror* then *Delight.*
This my Chamber of *Neglect,*
Wall'd about with *Difrefpect,*
From all thefe and this dull ayre,
A fit obiect for *Defpaire,*
She hath taught me by her might
To draw comfort and delight.
Therefore *thou beft earthly bliffe,*
I will cherifh thee for this.
Poefie; thou fweeteft content
That e're Heau'n to mortals lent:
Though they as a trifle leaue thee
Whofe dull thoughts cannot conceiue thee,

M m 2   Though

The Shepheards Hunting.

Though thou be to them a fcorne,
That to nought but earth are borne:
Let my life no longer be
Then I am in loue with thee.
Though our wife ones call thee madneffe
Let me neuer tafte of gladneffe.
If I loue not thy mad'ft fits,
More then all their greateft wits.
And though fome too feeming holy,
Doe account thy raptures folly:
Thou doft teach me to contemne,
What make *Knaues* and *Fooles* of them.
Oh high power! that oft doth carry
Men aboue————————.

     Willie.

————Good *Philarete* tarry,
I doe feare thou wilt be gon,
Quite aboue my reach anon.
The kinde flames of Poefie
Haue now borne thy thoughts fo high,
That they vp in Heauen be,
And haue quite forgotten me.
Call thy felfe to minde againe,
Are thefe Raptures for a Swaine,
That attends on lowly Sheepe,
And with fimple Heards doth keepe?

         Philarete.

The Shepheards Hunting.

Philarete.

Thankes my *Willie*; I had runne
Till that Time had lodg'd the Sunne,
If thou had'ſt not made me ſtay;
But thy pardon here I pray.
Lou'd *Apolo's* ſacred fire
Had rais'd vp my ſpirits higher
Through the loue of Poeſie,
Then indeed they vſe to flye.
But as I ſaid, I ſay ſtill,
If that I had *Willi's* skill,
Enuie nor Detractions tongue,
Should ere make me leaue my ſong:
But I'de ſing it euery day
Till they pin'd themſelues away.
Be thou then aduis'd in this,
Which both iuſt and fitting is:
Finiſh what thou haſt begun,
Or at leaſt ſtill forward run.
Haile and Thunder ill hee'l beare
That a blaſt of winde doth feare:
And if words will thus afray thee,
Prethee how will deeds diſmay thee?
Doe not thinke ſo rathe a *Song*
Can paſſe through the vulgar throng,
And eſcape without a touch,
Or that they can hurt it much:

The Shepheards Hunting.

Frosts we see doe nip that thing
Which is forward'st in the Spring:
Yet at last for all such lets
Somewhat of the rest it gets.
And I'me sure that so maist thou,
Therefore my kind *Willie* now.
Since thy folding time drawes on
And I see thou must be gon,
Thee I earnestly beseech
To remember this my speech
And some little counsell take,
For *Philarete* his sake:
And I more of this will say,
If thou come next Holy-day.

FINIS.

The Shepheards Hunting.

The fifth Eglogue.

THE ARGVMENT.
Philaret Alexis *moues*,
To embrace the Mufes *loues*;
Bids him neuer carefull feeme,
Of anothers dif-efteeme:
Since to them it may fuffice,
They themfelues can iuftly prize.

PHILARETE. ALEXIS.

Philarete.

A *Lexis*, if thy worth doe not difdaine
The humble friendfhip of a meaner Swaine,
Or fome more needfull bufineffe of the day,
Vrge thee to be too hafty on thy way;
Come (gentle Shepheard) reft thee here by mee,
Beneath the fhadow of this broad leau'd tree:
For though I feeme a ftranger, yet mine eye
Obferues in thee the markes of courtefie:

Mm 4 And

The Shepheards Hunting.

And if my iudgement erre not, noted to,
More then in thofe that more would feeme to doe.
Such *Vertues* thy rare modefty doth hide.
Which by their proper lufter I efpy'd ;
And though long maskt in filence they haue beene,
I haue a Wifedome through that filence feene,
Yea, I haue learned knowledge from thy tongue,
And heard when thou haft in concealement fung.
Which me the bolder and more willing made
Thus to inuite thee to this homely fhade.
And though (it may be) thou couldft neuer fpie,
Such worth in me, I might be knowne thereby :
In thee I doe ; for here my neighbouring Sheepe
Vpon the border of thefe Downes I keepe :
Where often thou at Paftorals and Playes,
Haft grac'd our Wakes on Summer Holy-dayes :
And many a time with thee at this cold fpring
Met I, to heare your learned fhepheards fing,
Saw them difporting in the fhady Groues,
And in chafte Sonnets wooe their chafter Loues :
When I, endued with the meaneft skill,
Mongft others haue been vrg'd to tune my quill.
But, (caufe but little cunning I had got)
Perhaps thou faw'ft me, though thou knew'ft me not.

Alexis.

Yes *Philaret*, I know thee, and thy name.
Nor is my knowledge grounded all on fame :

Art

The Shepheards Hunting.

Art thou not he, that but this other yeere,
Scard'ſt all the Wolues and Foxes in the Sheere?
And in a match at Foot-ball lately tride
(Hauing ſcarce twenty Satyrs on thy ſide)
Held'ſt play : and though aſſailed kept'ſt thy ſtand
Gainſt all the beſt-tride Ruffians in the Land?
Did'ſt thou not then in dolefull Sonnets mone,
When the beloued of great *Pan* was gone?
And at the wedding of faire *Thame* and *Rhine*,
Sing of their glories to thy Valentine?
I know it, and I muſt confeſſe that long
In one thing I did doe thy nature wrong :
For, till I mark'd the ayme thy Satyrs had,
I thought them ouer-bold, and thee halfe mad.
But, ſince I did more neerely on thee looke,
I ſoone perceiu'd that I all had miſtooke ;
I ſaw that of a *Cynicke* thou mad'ſt ſhow,
Where ſince, I finde, that thou wert nothing ſo ;
And that of many thou much blame had'ſt got,
When as thy *Innocency* deſeru'd it not.
But that too good opinion thou haſt ſeem'd
To haue of me (not ſo to be eſteem'd,)
Preuailes not ought to ſtay him who doth feare,
He rather ſhould reproofes then prayſes heare.
'Tis true, I found thee plaine and honeſt to,
Which made mee like, then loue, as now I do ;
And, *Phila*, though a ſtranger, this to thee Ile ſay,
Where I doe loue, I am not coy to ſtay.
                                                    Phil.

The Shepheards Hunting.

Philarete.

Thankes, gentle Swaine, that doſt ſo ſoone vnfold
What I to thee as gladly would haue told:
And thus thy wonted curteſie expreſt
In kindly entertaining this requeſt.
Sure, I ſhould iniure much my owne content,
Or wrong thy loue to ſtand on complement:
Who haſt acquaintance in one word begun,
As well as I could in an age haue done.
Or by an ouer-weaning ſlowneſſe marre
What thy more wiſdome hath brought on ſo farre.
Then ſit thou downe, and Ile my minde declare,
As freely, as if we familiars were:
And if thou wilt but daigne to giue me eare,
Something thou mayſt for thy more profit heare.

Alexis.

Philarete, I willingly obey.

Philarete.

Then know, *Alexis*, from that very day,
When as I ſaw thee at thy Shepheards Coate,
Where each (I thinke) of other tooke firſt note;
I meane that Paſtor who by *Tauies* ſprings,
Chaſte Shepheards loues in ſweeteſt numbers ſings,
And with his Muſicke (to his greater fame)
Hath late made proud the faireſt *Nymphs* of Thame.
                                                                E'ne

The Shepheards Hunting.

E'ne then (me thought) I did efpy in thee
Some vnperceiu'd and hidden worth to bee:
Which, in thy more apparant vertues, fhin'd ;
And, among many, I (in thought) deuin'd,
By fomething my conceit had vnderftood,
That thou wert markt one of the *Mufes* brood,
That, made me loue thee: and that Loue I beare
Begat a Pitty, and that Pitty, Care :
Pitty I had to fee good parts conceal'd,
Care I had how to haue that good reueal'd,
Since 'tis a fault admitteth no excufe,
To poffeffe much, and yet put nought in vfe.
Hereon I vow'd (if wee two euer met)
The firft requeft that I would ftriue to get,
Should be but this, that thou would'ft fhew thy skill,
How thou could'ft tune thy Verfes to thy quill :
And teach thy *Mufe* in fome well-framed Song,
To fhew the *Art* thou haft fuppreft fo long:
Which if my new-acquaintance may obtaine,
I will for euer honour this daies gaine.

Alexis.

Alas ! my fmall experience fcarce can tell,
So much as where thofe *Nymphs*, the *Mufes*, dwell ;
Nor (though my flow conceit ftill trauels on)
Shall I ere reach to drinke of *Hellicon*.
Or, if I might fo fauour'd be to tafte
What thofe fweet ftreames but ouer-flow in wafte,
                                                And

The Shepheards Hunting.

And touch *Parnaffus*, where it low'ſt doth lie,
I feare my skill would hardly flag ſo hie.

Philarete.

Deſpaire not Man, the Gods haue prized nought
So deere, that may not be with labour bought:
Nor need thy paine be great, ſince *Fate* and *Heauen*,
That (as a bleſſing) at thy birth haue giuen.

Alexis.

Why, ſay they had?————————

Philarete.

————————Then vſe their gifts thou muſt.
Or be vngratefull, and ſo be vnjuſt:
For if it cannot truely be deni'd,
Ingratitude mens benefits doe hide;
Then more vngratefull muſt he be by ods,
Who doth conceale the bounty of the Gods.

Alexis.

That's true indeed, but *Enuy* haunteth thoſe
Who ſeeking Fame, their hidden skill diſcloſe:
Where elſe they might (obſcur'd) from her eſpying,
Eſcape the blaſts and danger of enuying:
Cryticks will cenſure our beſt ſtraines of Wit,
And pur-blind *Ignorance* miſconſter it.
                                                And

The Shepheards Hunting.

And which is bad, (yet worſe then this doth follow)
Moſt hate the *Muſes*, and contemne *Apollo*.

Philarete.

So let them: why ſhould wee their hate eſteeme?
Is't not enough we of our ſelues can deeme?
'Tis more to their diſgrace that we ſcorne them,
Then vnto vs that they our Art contemne.
Can we haue better paſtime then to ſee
Their groſſe heads may ſo much deceiued bee,
As to allow thoſe doings beſt, where wholly
We ſcoffe them to their face, and flout their folly?
Or to behold blacke *Enuy* in her prime,
Die ſelfe-conſum'd, whilſt we vie liues with time:
And, in deſpight of her, more fame attaine,
Then all her malice can wipe out againe?

Alexis.

Yea, but if I appli'd mee to thoſe ſtraines,
Who ſhould driue forth my Flocks vnto the plaines,
Which, whil'ſt the *Muſes* reſt, and leaſure craue,
Muſt watering, folding, and attendance haue?
For if I leaue with wonted care to cheriſh
Thoſe tender *heards*, both I and they ſhould periſh.

Philarete.

Alexis, now I ſee thou doſt miſtake,
There is no meaning thou thy Charge forſake;

            Nor

The Shepheards Hunting.

Nor would I wifh thee fo thy felfe abufe,
As to neglect thy calling for thy *Mufe*.
But, let thefe two, fo each of other borrow,
That they may feafon mirth, and leffen forrow.
Thy Flocke will helpe thy charges to defray,
Thy *Mufe* to paffe the long and teadious day:
Or whilft thou tun'ft fweet meafures to thy *Reed*,
Thy Sheepe, to liften, will more neere thee feed;
The Wolues will fhun them, birds aboue thee fing,
And Lamkins dance about thee in a Ring.
Nay, which is more; in this thy low eftate,
Thou in contentment fhalt with Monarks mate:
For mighty *Pan*, and *Ceres*, to vs grants,
Our Fields and Flocks fhall helpe our outward wants:
The *Mufes* teach vs Songs to put off cares,
Grac'd with as rare and fweet conceits as theirs:
And we can thinke our Laffes on the Greenes
As faire, or fairer, then the faireft Queenes:
Or, what is more then moft of them fhall doe,
Wee'le make their iufter fames laft longer to,
And haue our Lines by greateft Princes grac'd
When both their name and memori's defac'd.
Therefore, *Alexis*, though that fome difdaine
The heauenly Muficke of the Rurall plaine,
What is't to vs, if they (o'refeene) contemne
The dainties which were nere ordain'd for them?
And though that there be other-fome enuy
The prayfes due to facred Poefie;

            Let

The Shepheards Hunting.

Let them difdaine, and fret till they are weary,
Wee in our felues haue that fhall make vs merry:
Which, he that wants, and had the power to know it,
Would giue his life that he might die a Poet.

Alexis.

A braue perfwafion.————————

Philarete.

————————Here thou fee'ft mee pent
Within the jawes of ftrict imprifonment;
A fore-lorne *Shepheard*, voyd of all the meanes,
Whereon Mans common hope in danger leanes:
Weake in my felfe, expofed to the *Hate*
Of thofe whofe *Enuies* are infatiate:
Shut from my friends, banifh'd from all delights;
Nay worfe, excluded from the facred *Rites*.
Here I doe liue mongft out-lawes markt for death,
As one vnfit to draw the common breath,
Where thofe who to be good did neuer know,
Are barred from the meanes fhould make them fo.
I fuffer, caufe I wifh'd my Country well,
And what I more muft beare I cannot tell.
I'me fure they giue my Body little fcope,
And would allow my *Minde* as little *Hope:*
I wafte my Meanes, which of it felfe is flender,
Confume my Time (perhaps my fortunes hinder)
And

The Shepheards Hunting.

And many Croſſes haue, which thoſe that can
Conceiue no wrong that hurts another man,
Will not take note of ; though if halfe ſo much
Should light on them, or their owne perſon touch,
Some that themſelues (I feare) moſt worthy thinke,
With all their helpes would into baſeneſſe ſhrinke.
But, ſpight of *Hate*, and all that Spight can do,
I can be patient yet, and merry to.
That ſlender *Muſe* of mine, by which my *Name*,
Though ſcarſe deſeru'd, hath gain'd a little fame,
Hath made mee vnto ſuch a Fortune borne,
That all misfortunes I know how to ſcorne ;
Yea, midſt theſe bands can ſleight the *Great'ſt* that bee,
As much as their diſdaine miſteemes of mee.
This Caue, whoſe very preſence ſome affrights,
I haue oft made to Eccho forth delights,
And hope to turne, if any Iuſtice be,
Both ſhame and care on thoſe that wiſh'd it me.
For while the World rancke villanies affords,
I will not ſpare to paint them out in words ;
Although I ſtill ſhould into troubles runne,
I knew what man could act, ere I begun ;
And I'le fulfill what my *Muſe* drawes mee to,
Maugre all *Iayles*, and *Purgatories* to.
For whil'ſt ſhee ſets mee honeſt task's about,
Vertue, or ſhee, (I know) will beare mee out :
And if, by *Fate*, th'abuſed power of ſome
Muſt, in the worlds-eye, leaue mee ouercome,
They

The Shepheards Hunting.

They shall find one Fort yet, so fenc'd I trow,
It cannot feare a Mortals ouer-throw.
This *Hope*, and *Trust*, that great power did infuse,
That first inspir'd into my brest a *Muse*,
By whom I doe, and euer will contemne
All those ill haps, my foes despight, and them.

Alexis.

Th'hast so well *(yong Philaret)* plaid thy part,
I am almost in loue with that sweet Art:
And if some power will but inspire my song,
Alexis will not be obscured long.

Philarete.

Enough kinde Pastor: But oh! yonder see
Two honest Shepheards walking hither, bee
Cuddy and *Willy*, that so dearely loue,
Who are repairing vnto yonder Groue:
Let's follow them: for neuer brauer Swaines
Made musicke to their flocks vpon these Plaines.
They are more worthy, and can better tell
What rare contents doe with a Poet dwell.
Then whiles our sheepe the short sweet grasse do sheare
And till the long shade of the hils appeare,
Wee'le heare them sing: for though the one be young,
Neuer was any that more sweetly sung.

A Postscript.

To the Reader.

F you haue read this, and receiued any content, I am glad, (though it bee not so much as I could wish you) *if you thinke it idle, why then I see wee are not likely to fall out; for I am iust of your minds; yet weigh it well before you runne too farre in your censures, lest this proue lesse barren of Wit, then you of courtesie. It is very true (I know not by what chance) that I haue of late been so highly beholding to* Opinion, *that I wonder how I crept so much into her fauour, and if I did thinke it worthie the fearing) I should be afraid that she hauing*

To the Reader.

hauing so vndeseruedly befriended mee beyond my Hope or expectation, will, vpon as little cause, ere long, againe picke some quarrell against mee; and it may bee, meanes to make vse of this, *which I know must needes come farre short of their expectation, who by their earnest desire of it, seem'd to be fore-possest with a farre better conceite, then I can beleeue it prooues worthy of. So much at least I doubted, and therefore loth to deceiue the world (though it often beguile me) I kept it to my selfe, indeed, not dreaming euer to see it published: But now, by the ouermuch perswasion of some friends, I haue been constrained to expose it to the generall view. Which seeing I haue done, somethings I desire thee to take notice of. First, that I am* Hee, *who to pleasure my friend,*

Nn 2   haue

A Postscript

haue fram'd my selfe a content out of that which would otherwise discontent mee. Secondly, that I haue coueted more to effect what I thinke truely honest in it selfe, then by a seeming shew of Art, to catch the vaine blastes of vncertaine Opinion. *This that I haue here written, was no part of my studie, but onely a recreation in imprisonment: and a trifle, neither in my conceit fitting, nor by me intended to bee made common; yet some, who it should seeme esteemed it worthy more respect then I did, tooke paines to coppy it out, vnknowne to mee, and in my absence got it both Authorized and prepared for the Presse; so that if I had not hindred it, last* Michaelmas-Tearme *had beene troubled with it. I was much blamed by some Friends for withstanding*

to the Reader.

ding it, to whoſe requeſt I ſhould more eaſily haue conſented, but that I thought (as indeed I yet doe) I ſhould thereby more diſparage my ſelfe, then content them. For I doubt J ſhall bee ſuppoſed one of thoſe, who out of their arrogant deſire of a little prepoſterous Fame, *thruſt into the world euery vnſeaſoned trifle that drops out of their vnſetled braines; whoſe baſeneſſe how much I hate, thoſe that know mee can witneſſe, for if I were ſo affected, I might perhaps preſent the World with as many ſeuerall* Poems, *as I haue ſeene yeeres; and iuſtly make my ſelfe appeare to bee the Author of ſome things that others haue ſhamefully vſurped and made vſe of as their owne. But I will be content other men ſhould owne ſome of thoſe Iſſues of the* Braine, *for J would*

A Postscript

would be loath to confesse all that might in that kinde call me Father. Neither shall any more of them, by my consent, in haft againe trouble the world, vnlesse I know which way to benefit it with lesse preiudice to my owne estate. And therefore if any of those lesse serious Poems *which are already disperst into my friends hands, come amongst you, let not their publication be imputed to me, nor their lightnesse be any disparagement to what hath been since more serious written, seeing it is but such stuffe as riper iudgements haue in their farre elder yeeres been much more guilty of.*

I know an indifferent Crittick *may finde many faults, as well in the flightnesse of this present* Subiect *, as in the erring from the true nature of an* Eglogue *: moreouer, it altogether concernes*

to the Reader.

cernes my self, which diuers may diflike. But neither can bee done on iuſt cauſe: The firſt hath bin anſwered already: The laſt might conſider that I was there where my owne eſtate was chiefly to bee looked vnto, and all the comfort I could miniſter vnto my ſelfe, little enough.

If any man deeme it worthy his reading I ſhall bee glad: if hee thinke his paines ill beſtow'd, let him blame himſelfe for medling with that concerned him not: I neither commended it to him, neither cared whether he read it or no; becauſe I know thoſe that were deſirous of it, will eſteeme the ſame as much as I expect they ſhould.

But it is not vnlikely, ſome wil thinke I haue in diuers places been more wanton (as they take it) then befitting a Satirict; yet their ſeuerity I feare not, becauſe

A Postscript, &c.

I am assured all that I euer yet did, was free from Obscænity: *neyther am I so* Cynical, *but that I thinke a modest expression of such amorous conceits as sute with Reason, will yet very well become my yeeres; in which not to haue feeling of the power of* Loue, *were as great an argument of much stupidity, as an ouer-sottish affection were of extreame folly. Lastly, if you thinke it hath not well answered the Title of the* Shepheards Hunting, *goe quarrell with the* Stationer, *who bid himselfe God-Father, and imposed the* Name *according to his owne liking; and if you, or hee, finde any faults, pray mend them.*

Valete.

FINIS.

FIDELIA:

BY

GEORGE WITHER.
GENT:

LONDON,

Printed by *T. S.* for *Iohn Budge*, dwelling in *Pauls*-
Church-yard, at the figne of the Greene
Dragon, 1622.

An Elegiacall Epiſtle of *Fidelia*,
to her vnconſtant Friend.

THE ARGVMENT.

This Elegiacall Epiſtle, *being a fragment of ſome greater Poeme, diſcouers the modeſt affections of a diſcreet and conſtant Woman, ſhadowed vnder the name of* Fidelia; *wherein you may perceiue the height of their Paſſions, ſo farre as they ſeeme to agree with reaſon, and keepe within ſuch decent bounds as beſeemeth their Sex, but further it meddles not. The occaſion ſeemes to proceed from ſome mutability in her friend, whoſe obiections ſhee heere preſuppoſing, confuteth, and in the perſon of him iuſtly vpbraideth all that are ſubiect to the like change, or fickleneſſe in minde. Among the reſt, ſome more weightie Arguments then are (perhaps) expected in ſuch a ſubiect, are briefly, and yet ſomewhat ſeriouſly handled.*

Ft I haue heard tel, and now for truth I finde,
Once out of ſight, and quickly out of minde.
And that it hath been rightly ſaid of old,
Loue that's ſoon'ſt hot, is euer ſooneſt cold.

                                                    Or

Fidelia.

Or elſe my teares at this time had not ſtain'd
The ſpotleſſe paper, nor my lines complain'd.
I had not, now, been forced to haue ſent
Theſe lines for *Nuncio's* of my diſcontent;
Nor thus, exchanged, ſo vnhappily,
My ſongs of Mirth, to write an Elegie.
But, now I muſt; and, ſince I muſt doe ſo,
Let mee but craue, thou wilt not flout my woe:
Nor entertaine my ſorrowes with a ſcoffe,
But, reade (at leaſt) before thou caſt them off.
And, though thy heart's too hard to haue compaſſion,
Oh blame not, if thou pitty not my *Paſſion*,
For well thou know'ſt (alas, that er'e 'twas knowne)
There was a time (although that time be gone)
I, that for this, ſcarce dare a beggar bee,
Preſum'd for more to haue commanded thee.
Yea, the *Day* was, (but ſee how things may change)
When thou, and I, haue not been halfe ſo ſtrange;
But oft embrac'd each other, gently greeting,
With ſuch kinde words, as *Turtle, Doue,* or *Sweeting*.
Yea, had thy meaning, and thoſe vowes of thine,
Prou'd but as faithfull, and as true as mine,
It ſtill had been ſo: for (I doe not faine)
I ſhould rejoyce it might be ſo againe.
But, ſith thy *Loue* growes cold, and thou vnkinde,
Be not diſpleas'd I ſomewhat breath my minde;
I am in hope, my words may proue a mirrour,
Whereon thou looking, may'ſt behold thine error.
          And

Fidelia.

And yet, the *Heauen*, and my sad heart doth know,
How griu'd I am, and with what feeling woe
My minde is tortured, to thinke that I
Should be the brand of thy disloyalty:
Or, liue to be the Author of a line
That shall be printed with a fault of thine;
(Since if that thou but slightly touched be,
Deepe wounds of griefe, and shame, it strikes in me:)
And yet I must: ill hap compels me to
What I nere thought to haue had cause to do.
And therefore, seeing that some angry *Fate*
Imposes on mee, what I so much hate:
Or, since it is so, that the Powers diuine
Mee *(miserable)* to such cares assigne;
Oh that *Loues* patron, or some sacred *Muse*,
Amongst my *Passions*, would such Art infuse,
My well-fram'd words, and aiery sighs might proue
The happy blasts to re-inflame thy loue.
Or, at least, touch thee with thy fault so neere,
That thou might'st see thou wrong'st, who held thee (deere:
Seeing, confesse the same, and so abhorre it,
Abhorring, pitty, and repent thee for it.
But *(Deare)* I hope that I may call thee so,
(For thou art deare to mee, although a foe)
Tell mee, is't true, that I doe heare of thee,
And, by thy absence, true appeares to bee?
Can such abuse be in the Court of *Loue*,
False and inconstant now, thou *Hee* should'st proue?
                                                    Hee

Fidelia.

He, that fo wofull, and fo penfiue fate,
Vowing his feruice at my feete of late?
Art thou that *quondam* louer, whofe fad eye
I feldome faw yet, in my prefence dry?
And from whofe gentle-feeming tongue I know
So many pitty-mouing words could flow?
Was't thou, fo foughtft my loue, fo feeking that
As if it had been all th'hadft aymed at?
Making me think thy *Paſſion* without ftaine,
And gently quite thee with my loue againe?
With this perfwafion I fo fairely plac'd it,
Nor *Time*, nor *Enuy*, fhould haue ere defac'd it?
Is't fo? haue I done thus much? and art thou
So ouer-cloyed with my fauours now?
Art wearied fince with louing, and eftranged
So far? Is thy affection fo much changed,
That I of all my hopes muft be deceyued,
And all good thoughts of thee be quite bereaued?
 Then true I finde, which long before this day
I fear'd my felfe, and heard fome wifer fay;
That there is nought on earth fo fweet, that can
Long relifh with the curious tafte of Man.
 Happy was I; yea, well it was with mee,
Before I came to be bewitch'd by thee.
I ioy'd the fweet'ft content that euer *Maid*
Poſſeſſed yet; and truely well-a-paid,
Made to my felfe (alone) as pleafant mirth
As euer any *Virgine* did on earth.
            The

Fidelia.

The melody I vf'd was free, and fuch
As that Bird makes, whom neuer hand did touch;
But, vn-allur'd, (with *Fowlers* whiftling) flies
Aboue the reach of humane treacheries.
   And (well I doe remember) often then
Could I reade o're the pollicies of men;
Difcouer what vncertainties they were;
How they would figh, looke fad, proteft, and fweare;
Nay, faigne to die, when they did neuer proue
The flendreft touch of a right-worthy loue:
But had chil'd hearts, whofe dulneffe vnderftood
No more of *Paffion*, then they did of good.
All which I noted well, and in my minde
(A generall humour amongft women-kinde)
This vow I made; (thinking to keepe it than)
That neuer the faire tongue of any man,
Nor his complaint, though neuer fo much grieu'd,
Should moue my heart to liking whil'ft I liu'd.
   But, who can fay, what fhe fhall liue to do?
I haue beleeu'd, and let in liking to,
And that fo farre, I cannot yet fee how
I may fo much as hope, to helpe it now;
Which makes mee thinke, what e're we *women* fay,
Another minde will come another day.
And that men may to things vnhop'd for clime,
Who watch but *Opportunity* and *Time*.
For 'tis well knowne, we were not made of clay,
Or fuch courfe, and ill-temper'd ftuffe as they.

                                                  For

Fidelia.

For he that fram'd vs of their flesh, did daigne
When 'twas at best, to new refine't againe.
Which makes vs euer since the kinder *Creatures*,
Of farre more flexible, and yeelding *Natures*.
And as wee oft excell in outward parts,
So wee haue nobler and more gentle hearts.
Which, you well knowing, daily doe deuise
How to imprint on them your *Cruelties*.
But doe I finde my cause thus bad indeed?
Or else on things imaginary feed?
Am I the lasse that late so truly iolly,
Made my selfe merry oft, at others folly?
Am I the Nymph that *Cupids* fancies blam'd,
That was so cold, so hard to be inflam'd?
Am I my selfe? or is my selfe that *Shee*
Who from this *Thraldome*, or such falshoods free,
Late own'd mine owne heart, and full merry then,
Did fore-warne others to beware of Men?
And could not, hauing taught them what to doe,
Now learne my selfe, to take heede of you to?
Foole that I am, I feare my guerdon's iust,
In that I knew this, and presum'd to trust.
And yet (alas) for ought that I could tell,
One sparke of goodnesse in the world might dwell:
And then, I thought, If such a thing might be,
Why might not that one sparke remaine in thee?
For thy faire out-side, and thy fayrer tongue,
Did *promise* much, although thy yeares were young.

                                               And

Fidelia.

And *Vertue* (wherefoeuer fhe be now)
Seem'd then, to fit enthron'd vpon thy brow.
Yea, fure it was: but, whether 'twere or no,
Certaine I am, and was perfwaded fo.
Which made me loth to thinke, that words of fafhion,
Could be fo fram'd, fo ouer-laid with *Paſſion* ;
Or fighes fo feeling, fain'd from any breft.
Nay, fay thou hadft been falfe in all the reft ;
Yet from thy eye, my heart fuch notice tooke,
Me thought, guile could not faine fo fad a looke.
But now I'ue try'd, my bought experience knowes,
They oft are worſt that make the faireſt ſhowes.
And howfoe're men faine an outward grieuing,
'Tis neither worth reſpecting, nor belieuing :
For, fhe that doth one to her mercy take,
Warmes in her bofome but a frozen fnake :
Which heated with her fauours, gather fence,
And ftings her to the heart in recompence.
 But tell me why, and for what fecret fpight
You in poore womens miferies delight ?
For fo it feemes ; elfe why d'yee labour for
That, which when 'tis obtained, you abhor ?
Or to what end doe you endure fuch paine
To win our loue, and caft it off againe ?
Oh that we either your hard hearts could borrow,
Or elfe your ftrengths, to helpe vs beare our forrow :
 But we are caufe of all this griefe and fhame,
And we haue none but our owne felues to blame :

    O o   For

Fidelia.

For still we see your falshood for our learning,
Yet neuer can haue power to tak't for warning;
But (as if borne to be deluded by you)
We know you trustlesse, and yet still we try you.
    (Alas) what wrong was in my power to doe thee?
Or what despight haue I er'e done vnto thee?
That thou shouldst chuse Me, aboue all the rest,
To be thy scorne, and thus be made a iest?
Must mens il natures such true villaines proue them,
To make thē wrong those most that most do loue them?
Couldst thou finde none in *Countrey*, *Towne* or *Court*,
But onely Me, to make thy *Foole*, thy sport?
Thou knowst I haue no wanton courses runne,
Nor seemed easie vnto lewdnesse wonne.
And (though I cannot boast me of much wit,)
Thou saw'st no signe of fondnesse in me yet.
Nor did ill nature euer so ore-sway me,
To flout at any that did woe or pray me,
But grant I had been guilty of abusage,
Of thee I'me sure I ne're deseru'd such vsage.
But thou wert grieued to behold my smilings,
When I was free from loue, and thy beguilings.
Or to what purpose else didst thou bestow
Thy time, and study to delude me so?
Hast thou good parts? and dost thou bend them all
To bring those that ne're hated thee in thrall?
Prethee take heed, although thou yet inioy'st them
They'l be tooke from thee, if thou so imploy'st them.
                                 For

Fidelia.

For though I wiſh not the leaſt harme to thee,
I feare, the iuſt *Heauens* will reuenged be.
Oh *!* what of *Mee* by this time had become,
If my deſires with thine had hapt to rome,
Or I, vnwifely, had confented to
What (ſhameleſſe*)* once thou didſt attempt to doe *?*
I might haue falne, by thoſe immodeſt trickes,
Had not ſome power beene ſtronger then my Sex.
And if I ſhould haue ſo been drawne to folly,
I ſaw thee apt enough to be vnholy.
Or if my weakeneſſe had beene prone to ſinne,
I poorely by thy ſtrength had ſuccour'd bin.
You Men make vs belieue you doe but try,
And that's your part, *(*you ſay*)* ours to deny.
Yet I much feare, if we through frailty ſtray,
There's few of you within your bounds will ſtay ;
But, maugre all your ſeeming *Vertue,* be
As ready to forget your ſelues, as we.
   I might haue fear'd thy part of loue not ſtrong,
When thou didſt offer me ſo baſe a wrong *:*
And that I after loath'd thee not, did proue
In mee ſome extraordinary *Loue.*
For ſure had any other but in thought,
Preſum'd vnworthily what thou haſt ſought,
Might it appeare, I ſhould doe thus much for him,
With a ſcarce reconciled hate abhorre him.
   My young experience neuer yet did know
Whether deſire might range ſo farre, or no,

Fidelia.

To make true *Louers* carelelly requeft,
What rafh enioyning makes them moft vnbleft,
Or blindly thorow frailty giue confenting
To that, which done brings nothing but repenting. .
But in my iudgement it doth rather proue
That they are fir'd with luft, then warm'd with loue.
And if it be for proofe men fo proceed,
It fhewes a doubt, elfe what doe tryals neede?
And where is that man liuing euer knew
That falfe diftruft, could be with loue that's true?
Since the meere caufe of that vnblam'd effect,
Such an opinion is, that hates fufpect.
   And yet, thee and thy loue I will excufe,
If thou wilt neither me, nor mine abufe.
For, Ile fuppofe thy paffion made thee proffer
That vnto me, thou to none elfe wouldft offer.
And fo, thinke thou, if I haue thee deni'd,
Whom I more lou'd then all men elfe befide;
What hope haue they, fuch fauour to obtaine,
That neuer halfe fo much refpect could gaine?
   Such was my loue, that I did value thee
Aboue all things below eternity.
Nothing on *Earth* vnto my heart was nearer
No Ioy fo prized, nor no Iewell dearer.
Nay: I doe feare I did *Idolatrize*;
For which *Heauens* wrath inflicts thefe miferies,
And makes the things which were for bleffings lent,
To be renewers of my difcontent.
                                      Where

Fidelia.

Where was there any of the *Naiades*,
The *Dryad's*, or the *Hamadryades*?
Which of the *Brittish* shires can yeeld againe,
A miftreffe of the Springs, or Wood, or Plaine?
Whofe eye enioy'd more fweet contents then mine,
Till I receiu'd my ouerthrow by thine?
Where's fhe did more delight in Springs and Rils?
Where's fhe that walk'd more Groues, or Downs, or Hils?
Or could by fuch faire artleffe profpect, more
Adde by conceit, to her contentments ftore
Then I; whilft thou wert true, and with thy Graces
Didft giue a pleafing prefence to thofe places?
But now *What is*? *What was* hath ouerthrowne,
My Rofe-deckt allies, now with Rue are ftrowne;
And from thofe flowers that honyed vfe to be,
I fucke nought now but iuyce to poyfon mee.

  For eu'n as fhe, whofe gentle fpirit can raife,
To apprehend *Loues* noble myfteries,
Spying a precious *Iewell* richly fet,
Shine in fome corner of her *Cabenet*,
Taketh delight at firft to gaze vpon
The pretty luftre of the fparkling ftone,
(And pleas'd in mind, by that doth feeme to fee
How vertue fhines through bafe obfcurity;)
But prying neerer, feeing it doth proue
Some relique of her deere deceafed *Loue*,
Which to her fad remembrance doth lay ope,
What fhe moft fought, and fees moft far from hope:

Fidelia.

Fainting almoſt beneath her *Paſſions* weight,
And quite forgetfull of her firſt conceit :
Looking vpon't againe, from thence ſhe borrowes
Sad melancholy thoughts to feed her ſorrowes.
   So I beholding *Natures* curious bowers,
Seel'd, ſtrow'd, and trim'd vp with leaues, hearbes, and
Walke pleaſed on a while, and doe deuize,   (flowers.
How on each obieƈt I may moralize.
But er'e I pace on many ſteps, I ſee
There ſtands a *Hawthorne* that was trim'd by thee :
Here thou didſt once ſlip off the virgin ſprayes,
To crowne me with a wreath of liuing Bayes.
On ſuch a Banke I ſee how thou didſt lye,
When viewing of a ſhady *Mulbery*,
The hard miſhap thou didſt to me diſcuſſe
Of louing *Thysbe*, and young *Piramus* :
And oh (thinke I) how pleaſing was it then,
Or would be yet, might he returne agen.
But if ſome neighbouring *Row* doe draw me to
Thoſe *Arbors*, where the ſhadowes ſeeme to wooe
The weary loue-ſicke *Paſſenger*, to ſit
And view the beauties *Nature* ſtrowes on it ;
How faire (thinke I) would this ſweet place appeare,
If he I loue, were preſent with me heere.
Nay, euery ſeuerall obieƈt that I ſee,
Doth ſeuerally (me thinkes) remember thee.
But the delight I vſ'd from thence to gather,
I now exchange for cares, and ſeeke them rather.
                                                But

Fidelia.

But thofe whofe dull and groffe affections can
Extend but onely to defire a *Man*,
Cannot the depth of thefe rare *Paffions* know:
For their imaginations flagge too low,
And caufe their bafe *Conceits* doe apprehend
Nothing but that whereto the flefh doth tend;
In *Loues* embraces they neere reach vnto
More of content than the brute *Creatures* do.
Neither can any iudge of this, but fuch
Whofe brauer mindes for brauer thoughts doe touch,
And hauing fpirits of a nobler frame,
Feele the true heate of *Loues* vnquenched flame.
 They may conceiue aright what fmarting fting
To their *Remembrances* the place will bring,
Where they did once enioy, and then doe miffe,
What to their foules moft deere and precious is.
With mee 'tis fo; for thofe walkes that once feem'd
Pleafing, when I of thee was more efteem'd,
To me appeare moft defolate and lonely,
And are the places now of torment onely.
Where I the higheft of contents did borrow,
There am I paid it home with deepeft forrow.
 Vnto one place, I doe remember well,
We walkt the eu'nings to heare *Phylomel*:
And that feemes now to want the light it had,
The fhadow of the *Groue's* more dull and fad,
As if it were a place but fit for Fowles,
That fcreech ill-lucke; as melancholy *Owles*,

Fidelia.

Or fatall *Rauens*, that feld' boding good,
Croke their blacke *Auguries* from fome darke wood.
   Then if from thence I halfe defpairing goe,
Another place begins another wo:
For thus vnto my thought it femes to fay,
Hither thou faw'ft him riding once that way:
Thither to meete him thou didft nimbly haft thee,
Yon he alighted, and eu'n there embrac'd thee:
Which whilft I fighing wifh to doe againe,
Another obiect brings another paine.
For paffing by that *Greene*, which (could it fpeake)
Would tell it faw vs run at *Barly-breake*;
There I beheld, what on a thin rin'd tree
Thou hadft engrauen for the loue of me;
When we two, all one in heate of day,
With chafte imbraces draue fwift houres away.
Then I remember to (vnto my fmart)
How loath we were, when time compel'd to part;
How cunningly thy *Paffions* thou couldft faine,
In taking leaue, and comming backe againe:
So oft, vntill (as feeming to forget
We were departing) downe againe we fet?
And frefhly in that fweet difcourfe went on,
Which now I almoft faint to thinke vpon.
   Viewing againe thofe other walkes and Groues
That haue beene witneffes of our chafte loues;
When I beheld thofe Trees whofe tender skin
Hath that cut out, which ftill cuts me within.
                                                                   Or

Fidelia.

Or come, by chance, vnto that pretty Rill
Where thou wouldſt ſit, and teach the neighbouring hill
To anſwere, in an Eccho, vnto thoſe
Rare *Problems* which thou often didſt propoſe.
When I come there (thinke I) if theſe could take
That vſe of words and ſpeech which we partake,
They might vnfold a thouſand pleaſures then
Which I ſhall neuer liue to taſte agen.
And thereupon, *Remembrance* doth ſo racke
My thoughts, with repreſenting what I lacke,
That in my minde thoſe Clerkes doe argue well,
Which hold *Priuation* the great'ſt plague of hell.
For there's no torment gripes mee halfe ſo bad,
As the *Remembrance* of thoſe joyes I had.
 Oh haſt thou quite forgot, when ſitting by
The bankes of *Thame*, beholding how the *Fry*
Play'd on the ſiluer-waues? There where I firſt
Granted to make my *Fortune* thus accurſt;
There where thy too-too earneſt ſuit compeld.
My ouer-ſoone beleeuing heart to yeeld
One fauour firſt, which then another drew
To get another, till (alas) I rue
That day and houre, thinking I nere ſhould need
(As now) to grieue for doing ſuch a deed.
So freely I my curteſies beſtow'd,
That whoſe I was vnwarily I ſhow'd:
And to my heart ſuch paſſage made for thee,
Thou canſt not to this day remoued be,
           And

Fidelia.

And what breaſt could reſiſt it, hauing ſeene
How true thy loue had in appearance beene?
For (I ſhall ne're forget) when thou hadſt there
Laid open euery diſcontent and care,
Wherewith thou deeply ſeem'dſt to me oppreſt,
When thou (as much as any could proteſt)
Had'ſt vow'd and ſworne, and yet perceiu'dſt no ſigne
Of pitty-mouing in this breſt of mine:
Well Loue (ſaid'ſt thou) ſince neither ſigh nor vow,
Nor any ſeruice may auaile me now:
Since neither the recitall of my ſmart,
Nor thoſe ſtrong *Paſſions* that aſſaile my heart;
Nor any thing may moue thee to beliefe
Of theſe my ſufferings, or to grant reliefe:
Since there's no comfort, nor deſert, that may
Get mee ſo much as *Hope* of what I pray;
Sweet *Loue* farewell; farewell faire beauties light,
And euery pleaſing obiect of the ſight:
My poore deſpayring heart heere biddeth you,
And all Content, for euermore, adue.
  Then eu'n as thou ſeemd'ſt ready to depart;
Reaching that hand, which after gaue my hart,
(And thinking this ſad *Farewell* did proceed
From a ſound breaſt, but truely mou'd indeed)
I ſtayed thy departing from mee ſo,
Whilſt I ſtood mute with ſorrow, thou for ſhow.
And the meane while as I beheld thy looke,
My eye th'impreſſion of ſuch *Pitty* tooke,
           That,

Fidelia.

That, with the ſtrength of *Paſſion* ouercome,
A deep-fetcht ſigh my heart came breathing from:
Whereat thou (euer wiſely vſing this
To take aduantage when it offered is)
Renewd'ſt thy ſute to mee, who did afford
Conſent, in ſilence firſt, and then in word.
    So that for yeelding thou maiſt thanke thy wit,
And yet when euer I remember it,
Truſt me, I muſe, and often (wondring) thinke,
Thorough what crancy, or what ſecret chinke
That *Loue*, vnwares, ſo like a ſlye cloſe Elfe,
Did to my heart inſinuate it ſelfe.
Gallants I had, before thou cam'ſt to woo,
Could as much loue, and as well court me to;
And, though they had not learned ſo the faſhion,
Of acting ſuch well counterfeited *Paſſion*;
In wit, and perſon, they did equall thee,
And worthier ſeem'd, vnleſſe thoul't faithfull be.
Yet ſtill vnmou'd, vnconquer'd I remain'd:
No, not one thought of loue was entertain'd:
Nor could they brag of the leaſt fauour to them,
Saue what meere curteſie enioyn'd to doe them.
Hard was my heart: But would't had harder bin,
And then, perhaps, I had not let thee in;
Thou, *Tyrant*, that art ſo imperious there,
And onely tak'ſt delight to *Dominere*.
But held I out ſuch ſtrong, ſuch oft aſſailing,
And euer kept the honour of preuailing?
                                    Was

Fidelia.

Was this poore-breaſt from loues allurings free,
Cruell to all, and gentle vnto thee?
Did I vnlocke that ſtrong affections dore,
That neuer could be broken ope before,
Onely to thee? and, at thy interceſſion,
So freely giue vp all my hearts poſſeſſion:
That to my ſelfe I left not one poore veine,
Nor power, nor will, to put thee from't againe?
Did I doe this, (and all on thy bare vow)
And wilt thou thus requite my kindneſſe now?
Oh that thou eyther hadſt not learn'd to faine,
Or I had power to caſt thee off againe!
How is it that thou art become ſo rude,
And ouer-blinded by *Ingratitude?*
Swar'ſt thou ſo deeply that thou wouldſt perſeuer,
That I might thus be caſt away for euer?
Well, then 'tis true, that Louers periuries,
Among ſome men, are thought no iniuries:
And that ſhe onely hath leaſt cauſe of griefe,
Who of your words hath ſmal'ſt, or no beliefe.
   Had I the wooer bin, or fondly won,
This had bin more tho, then thou couldſt haue don;
But, neither being ſo, what Reaſon is
On thy ſide, that ſhould make thee offer this?
   I know, had I beene falſe, or my faith fail'd,
Thou wouldſt at womens fickleneſſe haue rail'd;
And if in mee it had an error bin,
In thee ſhall the ſame fault be thought no ſin?
                                           Rather

Fidelia.

Rather I hold that which is bad in mee,
Will be a greater blemiſh vnto thee:
Becauſe, by *Nature*, thou art made more ſtrong,
And therefore abler to endure a wrong.
But 'tis our *Fortune*, you'le haue all the power,
Onely the *Care* and *Burden* muſt be our.
Nor can you be content a wrong to do,
Vnleſſe you lay the blame vpon vs to.
Oh that there were ſome gentle-minded *Poet*
That knew my heart, as well as now I know it;
And would endeare me to his loue ſo much,
To giue the world (though but) a ſlender touch
Of that ſad *Paſſion* which now clogs my heart,
And ſhew my truth, and thee how falſe thou art:
That all might know, what is beleeu'd by no man,
There's fickleneſſe in men, and faith in woman.

    Thou ſaw'ſt I firſt let *Pitty* in, then liking,
And laſtly, that which was thy onely ſeeking:
And, when I might haue ſcorn'd that loue of thine,
(As now vngently thou deſpiſeſt mine,)
Among the inmoſt Angles of my breſt,
To lodge it by my heart I thought it beſt:
Which thou haſt ſtolne to, like a thankeleſſe Mate,
And left mee nothing but a blacke ſelfe-hate.
What canſt thou ſay for this, to ſtand contending?
What colour haſt thou left for thy offending?
Thy wit, perhaps, can ſome excuſe deuiſe,
And faine a colour for thoſe iniuries;
                              But

Fidelia.

But well I know, if thou excuse this treason,
It must be by some greater thing then reason.
   Are any of those *vertues* yet defac'd,
On which thy first affection seemed plac'd?
Hath any secret foe my true faith wronged,
To rob the blisse that to my heart belonged?
What then? shall I condemned be vnheard,
Before thou knowest how I may be clear'd?
Thou art acquainted with the times condition,
Know'st it is full of enuy, and suspition,
So that the war'est in thought, word, and action,
Shall oft be iniur'd, by foule-mouth'd detraction:
And therefore thou (me-thinkes) should'st wisely pause
Before thou credit rumors without cause.
But I haue gotten such a confidence
In thy opinion, of my innocence:
It is not that, I know, with-holds thee now,
Sweet, tell mee then; is it some sacred vow?
Hast thou resolued, not to ioyne thy hand
With any one in *Hymens* holy band?
Thou shouldst haue done it then, when thou wert free,
Before thou hadst bequeath'd thy selfe to mee.
What vow dost deeme more pleasing vnto *Heauen*,
Then what is by vnfained louers giuen?
If any be, yet sure it frowneth at
Those that are made for contradicting that.
But, if thou wouldst liue chastely all thy life,
That thou maist do, though we be *man* and *wife:*
                                                Or,

Fidelia.

Or, if thou long'ſt a *Virgin*-death to die,
Why (if it be thy pleaſure) ſo doe I.
Make mee but thine, and I'le (contented) be
A *Virgin* ſtill, yet liue and lie with thee.
Then let not thy inuenting braine aſſay
To mocke, and ſtill delude mee euery way;
But call to minde, how thou haſt deepely ſworne
Not to neglect, nor leaue mee thus forlorne.
And if thou wilt not be to mee as when
Wee firſt did loue, doe but come ſee mee then.
Vouchſafe that I may ſometime with thee walke,
Or ſit and looke on thee, or heare thee talke;
And I that moſt content once aymed at,
Will thinke there is a world of bliſſe in that.
 Doſt thou ſuppoſe that my *Deſires* denies
With thy affections well to ſympathize?
Or ſuch peruerſneſſe haſt thou found in me,
May make our *Natures* diſagreeing be?
Thou knowſt when thou didſt wake I could not ſleepe;
And if thou wert but ſad, that I ſhould weepe.
Yet (euen when the teares my cheeke did ſtaine)
If thou didſt ſmile, why I could ſmile againe:
I neuer did contrary thee in ought:
Nay, thou canſt tell, I oft haue ſpake thy thought.
Waking; the ſelfe-ſame courſe with thee I runne,
And ſleeping, oftentimes our dreames were one.
 The Dyall-needle, though it ſence doth want,
Still bends to the beloued *Adamant*;

            Life

Fidelia.

Lift the one vp, the other vpward tends;
If this fall downe, that prefently defcends:
Turne but about the ftone, the fteele turnes to;
Then ftraight returnes, if fo the other do;
And, if it ftay, with trembling keepes one place,
As if it (panting) long'd for an imbrace.
So was't with mee: for, if thou merry wert,
That mirth of thine, mou'd ioy within my heart:
I fighed to, when thou didft figh or frowne:
When thou wert ficke, thou haft perceiu'd me fwoone;
And being fad, haue oft, with forc'd delight,
Striu'd to giue thee content beyond my might.
When thou wouldft talke, then haue I talk'd with thee,
And filent been, when thou wouldft filent be.
If thou abroad didft goe, with ioy I went;
If home thou lou'dft, at home was my content:
Yea, what did to my *Nature* difagree,
I could make pleafing, caufe it pleafed thee.
   But, if't be either my weake Sex, or youth,
Makes thee mifdoubt my vndiftained truth,
Know this; as none (till that vnhappy hower,
When I was firft made thine,) had euer power
To moue my heart, by vowes, or teares expence;
No more (I fweare) could any *Creature* fince.
No lookes but thine, though aim'd with *Paffions* Art,
Could pierce fo deepe to penetrate my hart.
No name but thine, was welcome to my eare;
No word did I fo foone, fo gladly heare:
Nor

Fidelia.

Nor euer could my eyes behold or fee,
What I was fince delighted in, but thee.
   And fure thou wouldft beleeue it to be fo,
If I could tell, or words might make thee know,
How many a weary night my tumbled bed
Hath knowne me fleepeleffe : what falt-teares I'ue fhed ;
What fcalding-fighes, the markes of foules oppreft,
Haue hourely breathed from my carefull breft.
Nor wouldft thou deeme thofe waking forrowes faind,
If thou mightft fee how fleeping I am paind.
For if fometimes I chance to take a flumber,
Vnwelcome dreames my broken reft doth cumber.
Which dreaming makes me ftart, ftarting with feares
Wakes ; and fo by waking I renew my cares :
Vntill my eyes ore-tir'd with watch and weeping,
Drownd in their owne flouds fall againe to fleeping.
Oh! that thou couldft but thinke, when laft wee parted,
How much I, grieuing for thy abfence, fmarted :
My very foule fell ficke, my heart to aking,
As if they had their laft *Farewels* beene taking ;
Or feared by fome fecret Diuination,
This thy reuolt, and caufeleffe alteration.
Didft thou not feele how loth that hand of mine,
Was to let goe the hold it had of thine ?
And with what heauy, what vnwilling looke
I leaue of thee, and then of comfort tooke ?
I know thou didft ; and though now thus thou doe,
I am deceiu'd, but then it grieu'd thee to.
            P p   Then,

Fidelia.

Then, if I fo with *Loues* fell paſſion vext
For thy departure onely was perplext,
When I had left to ſtrengthen me fome truſt;
And hope, that thou wouldſt nere haue prou'd vniuſt:
What was my torture then, and hard endurance,
When of thy falſhood I receiu'd aſſurance.
    Alas, my Tongue, a-while, with griefe was dumbe,
And a cold ſhuddering did my ioynts benumme,
Amazement feiz'd my thought, and fo preuailed,
I found me ill, but knew not what I ailed.
Nor can I yet tell, fince my fuffering then
Was more then could be ſhowne by *Poets* Pen;
Or well conceiu'd by any other hart
Then that which in fuch care hath borne a part.
    Oh me; how loth was I to haue beleeu'd
That to be true, for which fo much I grieu'd?
How gladly would I haue perſwaded bin,
There had bin no fuch matter, no fuch fin.
I would haue had my heart thinke that (I knew
To be the very truth) not to be true.
Why may not this, thought I, fome viſion be,
Some ſleeping dreame, or waking phantaſie,
Begotten by my ouer-blinded folly,
Or elſe engendred through my *Melancholy?*
But finding it fo reall (thought I) then
Muſt I be caſt from all my hopes agen?
What are become of all thofe fading bliſſes,
Which late my hope had, and now fo much miſſes?
                                    Where

Fidelia.

Where is that future fickle happineſſe
Which I ſo long expected to poſſeſſe?
And, thought I to; where are his dying *Paſſions*,
His honied words, his bitter lamentations?
To what end were his *Sonnets*, *Epigrams*,
His pretty *Poſies*, witty *Anagrams*?
I could not thinke, all that might haue been ſain'd,
Nor any faith, I thought ſo firme, bin ſtain'd.
Nay, I doe ſure and confidently know,
It is not poſſible it ſhould be ſo:
If that rare Art and *Paſſion* was thine owne,
Which in my preſence thou haſt often ſhowne.
But, ſince thy change, my much-preſaging heart
Is halfe afraid, thou ſome impoſtor wert:
Or that thou didſt but (Player-like addreſt)
Act that which flow'd from ſome more gentle breſt.
Thy puſt inuention, with worſe matter ſwolne,
Thoſe thy conceits from better wits hath ſtolne:
Or elſe (I know) it could not be, that thou
Shouldſt be ſo ouer-cold as thou art now;
Since thoſe, who haue that, feelingly, their owne,
Euer poſſeſſe more worth conceal'd, then knowne.
And if *Loue* euer any Mortals touch,
To make a braue impreſſion, 'tis in ſuch,
Who ſworne loues Chaplaines, will not violate
That, whereunto themſelues they conſecrate.
    But oh you noble brood, on whom the World
The ſlighted burthen of neglect hath hurl'd,

Pp 2   (Becauſe

Fidelia.

*(*Becaufe your thoughts for higher obiects borne,
Their groueling humors and affection fcorne*)*
You, whom the *Gods*, to heare your ftraines, will follow,
Whilft you doe court the fifters of *Apollo*.
You, whom there's none that's worthy, can neglect,
Or any that vnworthy is, affect.
Oh let not thofe that feeke to doe you fhame,
Bewitch vs with thofe fongs they cannot frame :
The nobleft of our Sexe, and faireft to,
Doe euer loue and honour fuch as you.
Then wrong vs not fo much to giue your *Paſſion*
To thofe that haue it but in imitation :
And in their dull breafts neuer feele the power
Of fuch deepe thoughts as fweetly moue in your.
As well as you, they vs thereby abufe,
For (many times) when we our *Louers* chufe,
Where we thinke *Nature*, that rich *Iewell*, fets
Which fhines in you, we light on counterfets.
    But fee, fee whither difcontentment beares me,
And to what vncoth ftraines my *Paſſion* reares me :
Yet pardon me, I here againe repent,
If I haue erred through that difcontent.
Be what thou wilt, be counterfeit or right,
Be conftant, ferious, or be vaine, or light,
My loue remaines inuiolate the fame,
Thou canft be nothing that can quench this flame,
But it will burne as long as thou haft breath
To keepe it kindled (if not after death*)*
                                                    Nere

Fidelia.

Nere was there one more true, then I to thee,
And though my faith muſt now deſpiſed be,
Vnpriz'd, vnualued at the loweſt rate,
Yet this Ile tell thee, 'tis not all thy ſtate,
Nor all that better-ſeeming worth of thine,
Can buy thee ſuch another *Loue* as mine :
Liking it may, but oh there's as much oddes,
Twixt loue and that, as betweene men and Gods.
It is a purchaſe not procur'd with treaſure,
As ſome fooles thinke, nor to be gaind at pleaſure :
For were it ſo, and any cou!d aſſure it,
What would not ſome men part with, to procure it ?
But though thou weigh't not, as thou ought'ſt to do,
Thou knowſt I loue ; and once didſt loue mee to.
Then where's the cauſe of this diſlike in thee ?
Suruey thy ſelfe, I hope there's none in mee.
Yet looke on her from whom thou art eſtranged ?
See, is my perſon, or my beauty changed ?
Once thou didſt praiſe it, prethee view't agen,
And marke ift be not ſtill the ſame twas then :
No falſe *Vermilion*-dye my cheeke diſtaines,
'Tis the poore bloud diſperſt through pores and vaines,
Which thou haſt oft ſeen through my fore-head fluſhing,
To ſhew no dawby-colour hid my bluſhing :
Nor neuer ſhall : *Vertue*, I hope, will ſaue mee,
Contented with that beauty *Nature* gaue mee.
Or, ift ſeeme leſſe, for that griefes-vaile had hid it,
Thou threwſt it on mee, 'twas not I that did it,

Fidelia.

    And canſt againe reſtore, what may repaire
All that's decay'd, and make me far more faire.
Which if thou doe, I'le be more wary than
To keep't for thee vnblemiſht, what I can:
And cauſe at beſt 'twill want much of perfection,
The reſt ſhall be ſupply'd with true affection.
    But I doe feare, it is ſome others riches,
Whoſe more abundance that thy minde bewitches,
That baſer obiect, that too generall aime,
Makes thee my leſſer *Fortune* to diſclaime.
Fie, canſt thou ſo degenerate in ſpirit,
As to prefer the meanes before the merit?
(Although I cannot ſay it is in mee)
Such worth ſometimes with pouerty may be
To equalize the match ſhe takes vpon her;
Tho th'other vaunt of *Birth, Wealth, Beauty, Honour:*
And many a one that did for greatneſſe wed,
Would gladly change it for a meaner bed.
Yet are my *Fortunes* knowne indifferent,
Not baſely meane, but ſuch as may content:
And though I yeeld the better to be thine,
I may be bold to ſay thus much, for mine;
That if thou couldſt of them and me eſteeme,
Neither thy ſtate, nor birth, would miſ-beſeeme:
Or if it did; how can I help't (alas)
Thou, not alone, before knew'ſt what it was.
But I (although not fearing ſo to ſpeed)
Did alſo diſinable't more than need,

                                  And

Fidelia.

And yet thou woo'dſt, and wooing didſt perſeuer,
As if thou hadſt intended *Loue* for euer :
Yea, thy account of wealth thou mad'ſt ſo ſmall,
Thou had'ſt not any queſtion of't at all ;
But hating much that peaſant-like condition,
Did'ſt ſeeme diſpleas'd I held it in ſuſpition.
Whereby I thinke, if nothing elſe doe thwart vs,
It cannot be the want of that will part vs.
Yea, I doe rather doubt indeed, that this
The needleſſe feare of friends diſpleaſure is.
Yes, that's the barre which ſtops out my delight,
And all my hope and ioy confoundeth quite.
But beares there any in thy heart ſuch ſway
To ſhut mee thence, and wipe thy loue away ?
Can there be any friend that hath the power,
To diſvnite hearts ſo conioyn'd as our ?
E're I would haue ſo done by thee ; I'de rather
Haue parted with one deerer then my father.
For though the will of our Creator bindes
Each Childe to learne and know his Parents mindes ;
Yet ſure I am, ſo iuſt a *Deitie,*
Commandeth nothing againſt *Pietie.*
Nor doth that band of duty giue them leaue,
To violate their faith, or to decciue.
And though that *Parents* haue authority,
To rule their children in minority :
Yet they are neuer granted ſuch power on them,
That will allow to tyrannize vpon them ;

Fidelia.

Or vfe them vnder their command fo ill,
To force them, without reafon, to their will.
    For who hath read in all the Sacred-writ,
Of any one compeld to marriage (yet ?)
What father fo vnkinde (thereto requir'd*)*
Denide his *Childe* the match that he defir'd,
So that he found the Lawes did not forbid it ?
I thinke thofe gentler ages no men did it.
In thofe daies therefore for them to haue bin
Contracted without licence had been fin ?
Since there was more good *Nature* among men,
And euery one more truly louing then.
But now (although we ftand obliged ftill
To labour for their liking, and good-will)
There is no duty whereby they may tie vs
From ought which without reafon they deny vs :
For I do thinke, it is not onely meant,
Children fhould aske, but *Parents* fhould confent :
And that they erre, their duty as much breaking,
For not confenting, as we not for fpeaking.
" It is no maruell many matches be
" Concluded now without their priuity ;
" Since they, through greedy *Auarice* mifled,
" Their intereft in that haue forfeited.
For, fome refpectleffe of all care, doe marry
Hot youthfull-*May*, to cold old-*Ianuary*.
Some, for a greedy end, doe bafely tie
The fweeteft-faire, to foule-deformitie.
                                    Forcing

Fidelia.

Forcing a loue from where 'twas placed late,
To re-ingraffe it where it turnes to hate.
It feemes no caufe of hindrance in their eyes,
Though manners nor affections fympathize.
And two Religions by their rules of ftate,
They may in one made body tolerate ;
As if they did defire that double ftemme,
Should fruitfull beare but *Neuters* like to them.
Alas, how many numbers of both kindes
By that haue euer difcontented mindes :
And liue (though feeming vnto others well)
In the next torments vnto thofe of hell ?
How many, defprate growne by this their finne,
Haue both vndone themfelues and all their kinne ?
Many a one, we fee, it makes to fall
With the too-late repenting *Prodigall.*
Thoufands (though elfe by nature gentler giuen,)
To act the horridft murthers oft are driuen.
And (which is worfe) there's many a carelefle elfe,
(Vnleffe Heauen pitty) kils and damnes his felfe.
Oh what hard heart, or what vnpittying eyes,
Could hold from teares to fee thofe Tragedies,
Parents, by their neglect in this, haue hurld
Vpon the Stage of this refpectleffe World ?
'Tis not one *Man*, one *Family*, one *Kinne*,
No nor one *Countrey* that hath ruin'd bin
By fuch their *folly*, which the caufe hath prou'd,
That forraine oft, and ciuill warres were mou'd
By

Fidelia.

By fuch beginnings many a City lies
Now in the duft, whofe *Turrets* brau'd the skies:
And diuers *Monarchs* by fuch fortunes croft,
Haue feene their Kingdomes fir'd, and fpoil'd, and loft.
    Yet all this while, thou feeft, I mention not,
The ruine, fhame, and chaftity hath got;
For 'tis a taske too infinite to tell
How many thoufands that would haue done well,
Doe, by the meanes of this, fuffer defires
To kindle in their hearts vnlawfull fires:
Nay fome, in whofe could breaft nere flame had bin,
Haue onely for meere vengeance falne to fin.
    My felfe haue feene, and my heart bled to fee't,
A wit-leffe Clowne enioy a match vnmeet.
She was a Laffe that had a looke to moue
The heart of cold *Diogenes* to loue:
Her eye was fuch, whofe euery glance did know
To kindle flames vpon the hils of Snow;
And by her powerfull piercings could imprint,
Or fparkle fire into a heart of flint:
And yet (vnleffe I much deceiued be)
In very thought did hate immodeftie.
And (had fh'enioyd the man fhe could haue lou'd)
Might, to this day, haue liued vn-reprou'd:
But, being forc'd, perforce, by feeming-friends,
With her confent, fhe her contentment ends.
In that, compel'd, her-felfe to him fhee gaue,
Whofe Bed, fhee rather could haue wifht her Graue;
                                            And

Fidelia.

And since, I heare, what I much feare is true,
That shee hath bidden shame and fame adue.
  Such are the causes now that *Parents* quite
Are put beside much of their ancient right:
Their feare of this, makes children to with-hold
From giuing them those dues which else they would:
And these thou fee'st are the too-fruitfull ils,
Which daily spring from their vnbridled wils.
Yet they, forsooth, will haue it vnderstood,
That all their study, is their childrens good.
A seeming-*Loue* shall couer all they do:
When, if the matter were well look't into,
Their carefull reach is chiefly to fulfill
Their owne soule, greedy, and insatiate will:
Who, quite forgetting they were euer young,
Would haue the Children dote, with them, on dung.
Grant, betwixt two, there be true loue, content,
Birth not mis-seeming, wealth sufficient,
Equality in yeares, an honest fame,
In euery-side the person without blame,
And they obedient too: What can you gather
Of Loue, or of affection, in that father,
That but a little to augment his treasure,
(Perhaps, no more but onely for his pleasure,)
Shall force his Childe to one he doth abhor,
From her he loues, and justly seeketh for;
Compelling him (for such mis-fortune grieu'd*)*
To die with care, that might with ioy haue liu'd?
                                     This

Fidelia.

This you may fay is *Loue*, and fweare as well,
There's paines in *Heauen*, and delights in *Hell*:
Or, that the Diuels fury and aufterity
Proceeds out of his care of our pofterity.
Would *Parents* (in this age) haue vs begin
To take by their eyes, our affections in?
Or doe they thinke we beare them in our fift,
That we may ftill remoue them as wee lift?
It is impoffible it fhould be thus,
For we are rul'd by *Loue*, not Loue by vs:
And fo our power fo much ner'e reached to,
To know where we fhall loue, vntill we doe.
And when it comes, hide it awhile wee may,
But 'tis not in our ftrengths to driu't away.

    Either mine owne eye fhould my chufer be,
Or I would ner'e weare *Hymens* Liuery.
For who is he fo neare my heart doth reft,
To know what 'tis, that mine approued beft?
I haue my felfe beheld thofe men, whofe frame
And outward perfonages had nought of blame:
They had (what might their good proportion grace)
The much more mouing part, a comely face,
With many of thofe complements, which we
In common men, of the beft breeding fee.
They had difcourfe, and wit enough to carry
Themfelues in fafhion, at an *Ordinary*;
Gallants they were, lou'd company and fport,
Wore fauours, and had *Miftreffes* in *Court*.

                                  And

Fidelia.

And euery way were such as well might seeme
Worthy of note, respect, and much esteeme;
Yet hath my eye more cause of liking seene,
Where nought perhaps by some hath noted beene:
And I haue there found more content, by farre,
Where some of these perfections wanting are;
Yea so much, that their beauties were a blot
To them (me thought) because he had them not.
    There some peculiar thing innated,
That beares an vncontrouled sway in this;
And nothing but it selfe knowes how to fit
The minde with that which best shall suit with it.
    Then why should *Parents* thrust themselues into
What they want warrant for, and power to doe?
How is it they are so forgetfull growne,
Of those conditions, that were once their owne?
Doe they so dote amidst their wits perfection,
To thinke that age and youth hath like affection?
(When they doe see 'mong those of equall yeares,
One hateth what another most endeares.)
Or doe they thinke their wisedomes can inuent
A thing to giue, that's greater than Content?
No, neither shall they wrap vs in such blindnesse,
To make vs thinke the spight they doe, is kindnesse.
For as I would aduise no childe to stray
From the least duty that he ought to pay:
So would I also haue him wisely know,
How much that duty is which he doth owe:
                                       That

Fidelia.

That knowing what doth vnto both belong,
He may doe them their right, himſelfe no wrong.
For if my *Parents* him I lothe ſhould chuſe,
Tis lawfull, yea my duty to refuſe :
Elſe, how ſhall I leade ſo vpright a life,
As is enioyned to the *Man* and *Wife?*
Since that we ſee ſometime there are repentings,
Eu'n where there are the moſt, and beſt contentings.
What, though that by our *Parents* firſt we liue?
Is not life miſery enough to giue ;
Which at their births the children doth vndo,
Vnleſſe they adde ſome other miſchiefe to?
Cauſe they gaue being to this fleſh of our,
Muſt we be therefore ſlaues vnto their power?
We nere defir'd it, for how could we tell,
Not being, but that not to be was well :
Nor know they whom they profit by it, ſeeing
Happy were ſome, if they had had no being.
Indeed, had they produc'd vs without ſin,
Had all our duty to haue pleas'd them bin :
Of the next life, could they aſſure the ſtate,
And both beget vs and regenerate ;
There were no reaſon then we ſhould withſtand
To vndergoe their tyrannou'ſt command :
In hope that either for our hard endurance,
We ſhould, at laſt, haue comfort in aſſurance :
Or, if in our endeauours we miſ-ſped,
At leaſt feele nothing when we ſhould be dead.
            But

Fidelia.

But what's the *Reaſon* for't that we ſhall be
Inthral'd ſo much vnto Mortality?
Our ſoules on will of any *Men* to tye
Vnto an euerlaſting miſery.
So farre, perhaps to, from the good of either,
We ruine them, our ſelues, and altogether.
 Children owe much, I muſt confeſſe 'tis true,
And a great debt is to the *Parents* due:
Yet if they haue not ſo much power to craue
But in their owne defence the liues they gaue:
How much leſſe then, ſhould they become ſo cruell
As to take from them the high-prized Iewell
Of liberty in choyce, whereon depends
The maine contentment that the heauen here lends?
Worth life, or wealth, nay far more worth then either
Or twenty thouſand liues put all together.
Then howſoeuer ſome, ſeuerer bent,
May deeme of my opinion, or intent,
With that which followes thus conclude I doe:
(And I haue Reaſon for't, and Conſcience to)
No Parent may his Childes iuſt ſute deny
On his bare will, without a reaſon why:
Nor he ſo vs'd, be diſobedient thought,
If vnapprou'd, he take the match he ſought.
 So then if that thy faith vncrazed be,
Thy friends diſlike ſhall be no ſtop to me:
For, if their will be not of force to doe it,
They ſhall haue no cauſe elſe to driue them to it.
           What

Fidelia.

What is it they againſt vs can alleage?
Both young we are, and of the fitteſt age,
If thou diſſembledſt not, both loue; and both
To admit hinderance in our loues are loth.
'Tis prejudiciall vnto none that liues;
And Gods, and humane Law our warrant giues.
Nor are we much vnequall in degree,
Perhaps our *Fortunes* ſomewhat different be.
But ſay that little meanes, which is, were not,
The want of wealth may not diſſolue this knot.
For though ſome ſuch prepoſterous courſes wend,
Preſcribing to themſelues no other end,
Marr'age was not ordain'd t'enrich men by,
Vnleſſe it were in their poſterity.
And he that doth for other cáuſes wed,
Nere knowes the true ſweetes of a marriage bed:
Nor ſhall he by my will, for 'tis vnfit
He ſhould haue bliſſe that neuer aym'd at it.
   Though that bewitching gold the *Rabble* blindes,
And is the obieƈt of all *Vulgar* mindes:
Yet thoſe, me-thinkes, that graced ſeeme to bee,
With ſo much good as doth appeare in thee,
Should ſcorne their better-taught deſires to tye
To that, which fooles doe get their honour by.
I can like of the wealth (I muſt confeſſe)
Yet more I prize the man, though mony-leſſe.
I am not of their humour yet, that can
For Title, or Eſtate, affeƈt a *Man*;
                                         Or

Fidelia.

Or of my felfe, one body deigne to make
With him I lothe, for his poffeffions fake.
Nor wifh I euer to haue that minde bred
In me, that is in thofe; who, when they wed,
Thinke it enough, they doe attaine the grace
Of fome new honour, to fare well, take place,
Weare coftly cloathes, in others fights agree,
Or happy in opinion feeme to bee.
   I weigh not this: for were I fure before
Of *Spencers* wealth, or our rich *Suttons* ftore;
Had I therewith a man, whom *Nature* lent,
Perfon enough to giue the eye content:
If I no outward due, nor right did want,
Which the beft Husbands in appearance grant:
Nay, though alone we had no priuate iarres
But merry liu'd from all domefticke cares;
Vnleffe I thought his *Nature* fo incline,
That it might alfo fympathize with mine,
(And yeeld fuch correfpondence with my mind'
Our foules might mutually contentment find,
By adding vnto thefe which went before,
Some certaine vnexpreffed pleafures more,
Such as exceed the ftreight and curb'd dimenfions
Of common mindes, and vulgar apprehenfions)
I would not care for fuch a match, but tarry
In this eftate I am, and neuer marry.
   Such were the fweets I hop'd to haue poffeft,
When *Fortune* fhould with thee haue made me bleft.
My heart could hardly thinke of that content,
To apprehend it without rauifhment.   Each

Fidelia.

Each word of thine (me-thought) was to my eares
More pleafing then that muficke, which the *Spheares*
(They fay) doe make the gods, when in their chime,
Their motions *Diapafon* with the time,
In my conceit, the opening of thine eye.
Seem'd to giue light to euery obiect by,
And fhed a kinde of life vnto my fhew,
On euery thing that was within it view.
More ioy I'ue felt to haue thee but in place,
Then many doe in the moft clofe embrace
Of their beloued'ft friend, which well doth proue,
Not to thy body onely tends my loue :
But mounting a true height, growes fo diuine,
It makes my foule to fall in loue with thine.
And fure now whatfoe're thy body doe,
Thy foule loues mine, and oft they vifit too.
For late I dream'd they went, I know not whither,
Vnleffe to *Heauen*, and there play'd together ;
And to this day I nere could know or fee,
'Twixt them or vs the leaft *Antipathy,*
Then what fhould make thee keepe thy perfon hence,
Or leaue to loue, or hold it in fufpence ?
If to offend thee I vnawares was driuen,
Is't fuch a fault as may not be forgiuen ?
Or if by frownes of *Fate,* I haue beene checkt,
So that I feeme not worth thy firft refpect,
Shall I be therefore blamed and vpbraided,
With what could not be holpen, or auoyded ?
Tis not my fault : yet caufe my *Fortunes* doe,
Wilt thou be fo vnkinde to wrong me too ?

                                          Not

Fidelia.

Not vnto *Thine*, but thee I fet my heart,
So nought can wipe my loue out while thou art :
Though thou wert poorer both of houfe and meat,
Then he that knowes not where to fleepe or eat ;
Though thou wert funke into obfcurity,
Become an abiect in the worlds proud eye,
Though by peruerfeneffe of thy *Fortune* croft,
Thou wert deformed, or fome limbe had'ft loft,
That loue which *Admiration* firft begot,
Pitty would ftrengthen, that it failed not :
Yea, I fhould loue thee ftill, and without blame,
As long as thou couldft keepe thy minde the fame ;
Which is of *Vertues* fo compact (I take it)
No mortall change fhall haue the power to fhake it.
This may, and will (I know) feeme ftrange to thofe
That cannot the *Abyfs* of loue difclofe,
Nor muft they thinke, whom but the out-fide moues
Euer to apprehend fuch noble *Loues* ;
Or more coniecture their vnfounded meafure,
Then can we mortals of immortall pleafure.
    Then let not thofe dull vnconceiuing braines,
Who fhall hereafter come to reade thefe ftraines,
Suppofe that no loues fire can be fo great,
Becaufe it giues not their cold Clime fuch heate ;
Or thinke m'inuention could haue reached here
Vnto fuch thoughts, vnleffe fuch loue there were :
For then they fhall but fhew their knowledge weake,
And iniure me, that feele of what I fpeake.
    But now my lines grow tedious, like my wrong,
And as I thought that, thou think'ft this too long.

                                                  Or

Fidelia.

Or some may deeme, I thrust my selfe into
More then beseemeth modesty to do.
But of the difference I am not vnwitting,
Betwixt a peeuish coynesse, and things fitting:
Nothing respect I, who pries ore my doing:
For here's no vaine allurements, nor fond wooing,
To traine some wanton stranger to my lure;
But with a thought that's honest, chaste, and pure,
I make my cause vnto thy conscience knowne,
Suing for that which is by right my owne.
In which complaint, if thou doe hap to finde
Any such word, as seemes to be vnkind:
Mistake me not, it but from *Passion* sprung,
And not from an intent to doe thee wrong.
Or if among these doubts my sad thoughts breed,
Some *(peraduenture)* may be more then need
They are to let thee know, might we dispute,
There,s no obiections but I could refute;
And spight of *Enuy* such defences make,
Thou shouldst embrace that loue thou dost forsake.
    Then do not (oh forgetfull man) now deeme,
That 'tis ought lesse then I haue made it seeme.
Or that I am vnto this *Passion* mou'd,
Becaufe I cannot else-where be belou'd:
Or that it is thy state, whose greatnesse knowne,
Makes me become a suter for my owne:
Suppose not so; for know this day there be
Some that wooe hard for what I offer thee:
And I haue euer yet contented bin
With that estate I first was placed in.
                                   Banish

Fidelia.

Banish thofe thoughts, and turne thee to my heart ;
Come once againe, and be what once thou wert.
Reuiue me by thofe wonted ioyes repairing,
That am nigh dead with forrowes and defpairing :
So fhall the memory of this annoy,
But adde more fweetneffe to my future ioy ;
Yea, make me thinke thou meantft not to deny me,
But onely wert eftranged thus, to try me.
And laftly, for that loues fake thou once bar'ft me,
By that right hand thou gau'ft, that oath thou fwar'ft me,
By all the *Paſſions*, and (if any be)
For her deare fake that makes thee iniure me ;
I here coniure thee ; no intreat and fue,
That if thefe lines doe ouer-reach thy view,
Thou wouldft afford me fo much fauour for them,
As to accept, or at leaft not abhorre them.
So though thou wholly cloake not thy difdaine,
I fhall haue fomewhat the leffe caufe to plaine :
Or if thou needs muft fcoffe at this, or me,
Do't by thy felfe, that none may witneffe be.
Not that I feare 'twill bring me any blame,
Onely I am loth the world fhould know my fhame.
For all that fhall this plaint with reafon view,
Will iudge me faithfull, and thee moft vntrue.
But if *Obliuion*, that thy loue bereft,
Hath not fo much good nature in thee left,
But that thou muft, as moft of you men doe,
When you haue conquer'd, tyrannize it too :
Know this before, that it is praife to no man
To wrong fo fraile a *Creature* as a woman.

Fidelia.

And to infult or'e one, fo much made thine,
Will more be thy difparagement then mine.
    But oh (I pray that it portend no harmes)
A chearing heate my chilled fenfes warmes :
Iuft now I flafhing feele into my breft,
A fudden comfort, not to be expreft ;
Which to my thinking, doth againe begin
To warne my heart, to let fome hope come in ;
It tels me 'tis impoffible that thou
Shouldft liue not to be mine, it whifpers how
My former feares and doubts haue beene in vaine,
And that thou mean'ft yet to returne againe.
It faies thy abfence from fome caufe did grow,
Which, or I fhould not, or I could not know.
It tels me now, that all thofe proofes, whereby
I feem'd affur'd of thy difloyalty,
May be but treacherous plots of fome bafe foes,
That in thy abfence fought our ouerthrowes.
    Which if it proue ; as yet me thinkes it may,
Oh, what a burden fhall I caft away ?
What cares fhall I lay by ? and to what height
Towre in my new afcenfion to delight ?
Sure er'e the full of it I come to try,
I fhall eu'n furfet in my ioy and die.
But fuch a loffe might well be call'd a thriuing
Since more is got by dying fo, then liuing.
    Come kill me then, my deare, if thou thinke fit,
With that which neuer killed woman yet :
Or write to me before, fo fhalt thou giue
Content more moderate that I may liue :
                                   And

Fidelia.

And when I see my staffe of trust vnbroken,
I will vnspeake againe what is mis-spoken.
What I haue written in dispraise of *Men*,
I will recant, and praise as much agen;
In recompence Ile adde vnto their Stories,
Encomiasticke lines to ymp their glories.
And for those wrongs my loue to thee hath done,
Both I and it vnto thy *Pitty* runne:
In whom, if the least guilt thou finde to be,
For euer let thine armes imprison me.
 Meane while I'le try if misery will spare
Me so much respite, to take truce with care.
And patiently await the doubtfull doome,
Which I expect from thee should shortly come;
Much longing that I one way may be sped,
And not still linger 'twixt aliue and dead.
For I can neither liue yet as I should,
Because I least enioy of that I would;
Nor quiet die, because (indeed) I first
Would see some better daies, or know the worst.
 Then hasten *Deare*, if to my end it be,
It shall be welcome, cause it comes from thee.
If to renew my *Comfort* ought be sent,
Let me not loose a minute of *Content*.
The precious *Time* is short, and will away,
Let vs enioy each other while we may.
Cares thriue, *Age* creepeth on, *Men* are but shades,
Ioyes lessen, *Youth* decaies, and *Beauty* fades;
New turnes come on, the old returneth neuer,
If we let our goe past, 'tis past for euer.
   FINIS.

A Metricall Paraphrafe

A Metricall Paraphrafe vpon
the CREEDE.

Ince it befits, that I account fhould giue
What way vnto faluation *I beleeue*;
Of my profeffion here the fumme I gather.
Firft, I confeffe a Faith *in God the Father:*
In God, who (without Helper or Pertaker)
Was of himfelfe the Worlds *Almighty Maker*,
And firft gaue Time his being: who gaue birth
To all the Creatures, both *of Heauen and Earth.*
Our euerlafting wel-fare doth confift
In his great mercies, *and in Iefus Chrift*:
*(*The fecond perfon of that Three in one*)*
The Father's equall, and *his onely Sonne*;
That euer-bleffed, and incarnate Word,
Which our Redeemer is, our life, *Our Lord.*
For when by Sathans guile we were deceiued,
Chrift was that meanes of helpe, *which was conceiued*;
Yea, (when we were in danger to be loft*)*
Conceiued for Vs, *by the Holy Ghoft.*
And that we might not euer be for-lorne,
For our eternall fafety he was *Borne*;
Borne as a Man (that Man might not mifcary*)*
Euen of the fubftance *of the Virgin Mary*,
And loe, a greater mercy, and a wonder;
He that can make All, fuffer, *fuffered vnder*

The

vpon the Creede.

The Iewish fpite (which all the world reuile at)
And Romish tyrannies of *Pontius Pilate.*
In him doe I beleeue, who was enuied,
Who with extreameſt hate *was Crucified*:
Who being Life it felfe (to make aſſured
Our foules of fafety) was both *dead, and buried*;
And that no feruile feare in vs might dwell,
To conquere, *Hee defcended into Hell*:
Where no infernall Power had power to lay
Command vpon him; but on *the third day*
The force of Death and Hell he did conſtraine;
And fo in Triumph, *He arofe againe.*
Yea, the Almighty power aduanc'd his head,
Afwell aboue all things, as *from the dead.*
Then, that from thence gifts might to men be giuen,
With glory, *Hee afcended into Heauen*:
Where, that fupreame and euerlaſting throne,
Which was prepar'd, he climb'd; *and fitteth on*
That bleſſed feate, where he fhall make abode
To plead for vs, at *the right hand of God.*
And no where fhould he be enthroned rather,
Then there: for, he is God, as is *the Father.*
And therefore, with an equall loue delight I
To praife and ferue them both, as one *Almighty*:
Yet in their office there's a difference.
And I beleeue, that Iefus Chriſt, *from thence,*
Shall in the great and vniuerfall doome,
Returne; and that with Angels *He ſhall come,*
To queſtion fuch as at his Empire grudge;
Euen thofe who haue prefumed him to *iudge.*

And

A Metricall Paraphrase

And that blacke day shall be so Catholicke,
As I beleeue not onely that *the quicke*
To that assise shall all be summoned;
But, he will both adiudge them, *and the dead.*
Moreouer, in the Godhead I conceiue
Another Person, in whom *I beleeue*:
For all my hope of blessednesse were lost,
If I beleeu'd not *in the holy Ghost.*
And though vaine Schismatickes through pride & folly
Contemne her power, I doe beleeue *the holy*
Chast Spouse of Christ (for whom so many search
By markes vncertaine) the true *Cath'like Church.*
I doe beleeue (God keepe vs in this vnion,)
That there shall be for euer *the Communion*
Of Gods Elect: and that he still acquaints
His Children in the fellowship *of Saints.*
Though damned be Mans naturall condition,
By grace in Christ I looke for *the remission*
Of all my foule misdeeds; for, there begins
Deaths end, which is the punishment *of sinnes.*
Moreouer, I the *Sadduces* infection
Abhorre, and doe beleeue *the Resurrection*:
Yea, though I turne to dust; yet through God, I
Expect a glorious rising *of the body*;
And that, exempted from the cares here rife,
I shall enioy perfection *and the life*
That is not subiect vnto change or wasting;
But euer-blessed, and for *euerlasting.*
This is my Faith, which that it faile not when
It most should steed me, let God say, *Amen.*

To

vpon the Lords Prayer.

To whom, that he so much vouchsafe me may,
Thus as a member of his Church, I pray:

Ord, at thy Mercy-feat, our selues we gather,
To doe our duties vnto thee, *Our Father.*
To whom all praise, al honor, should be giuen:
For, thou art that great God *which art in heauē.*
Thou by thy wisdome rul'st the worlds whole frame,
For euer, therefore, *Hallowed be thy Name.*
Let neuer more delayes diuide vs from
Thy glories view, but let *Thy Kingdome come.*
Let thy commands opposed be by none,
But thy good pleasure, and *Thy will be done.*
And let our promptnesse to obey, be euen
The very same *in earth, as 'tis in heauen.*
Then, for our selues, O Lord, we also pray,
Thou wouldst be pleased to *Giue vs this day,*
That food of life wherewith our soules are fed,
Contented raiment, and *our daily bread.*
With eu'ry needfull thing doe thou relieue vs:
And, of thy mercy, pitty *And forgiue vs*
All our misdeeds, in him whom thou didst please,
To take in offering for *our trespasses.*
And for as much, O Lord, as we beleeue,
Thou so wilt pardon vs, *as we forgiue*;
Let that loue teach vs, wherewith thou acquaints vs,
To pardon all *them, that trespasse against vs.*
                                        And

A Metricall Paraphrase, &c.

And though fometime thou findſt we haue forgot
This Loue, or thee; yet helpe, *And leade vs not* ⎫ *See*
Through Soule or bodies want, to defperation ⎬ *Pro.*
Nor let abundance driue, *into temptation.* ⎭ *30. 8. 9.*
Let not the foule of any true Beleeuer,
Fall in the time of tryall : *But deliuer*
Yea, faue him from the malice of the Diuell ;
And both in life and death keepe *vs from euill.*
Thus pray we Lord : And but of thee, from whom
Can this be had ? *For thine is the Kingdome.*
The world is of thy workes the grauen ſtory,
To thee belongs *the power, and the glory.*
And this thy happineſſe hath ending neuer :
But ſhall remaine *for euer, and for euer.*
This we confeſſe ; and will confeſſe agen,
Till we ſhall ſay eternally, *Amen.*

*Thou ſhalt write them vpon the poſtes of thy houſe,
and vpon thy Gates.* Deut. 6. 9.

FINIS.

Spenser Society.

LIST OF MEMBERS, 1870–71.

ADAMS, Dr. Ernest, Anson road, Victoria park, Manchester
Addis, John, jun., Rustington, Littlehampton, Sussex
Ainsworth, R. F., M.D., Higher Broughton, Manchester
Aitchison, William John, 11, Buckingham terrace, Edinburgh.
Akroyd, Colonel Edward, M.P., Halifax
Alexander, John, 43, Campbell street, Glasgow
Alexander, Walter, 29, St. Vincent place, Glasgow

BAIN, James, 1, Haymarket, London, S.W.
Baker, Charles, F.S.A., 11, Sackville street, London, W.
Baltimore, Peabody Institute at (per Mr. E. G. Allen, 12, Tavistock row, Covent garden, London, W.C.)
Barker, Philip, Birch Polygon, Rusholme, Manchester
Beard, James, The Grange, Burnage lane, Manchester
Bidder, George P., 131, Market street, Manchester
Birmingham Central Free Library
Birmingham Library (per Mr. A. Dudley, librarian)
Blackman, Frederick, 4, York road, London, S.E.
Bladon, James, Albion house, Pontypool
Boston, U.S., Athenæum (per Mr. E. G. Allen)
Boston, U.S., Public Library (per Sampson Low, Son and Co.)
Bremner, John A., Albert street, Manchester, *Hon. Sec.*
Brooks, W. Cunliffe, M.A., F.S.A., Barlow hall, near Manchester
Brothers, Alfred, 14, St. Ann's square, Manchester
Buckley, Rev. William Edward, M.A., Rectory, Middleton Cheney, Banbury

CALLENDER, William Romaine, jun., F.S.A., Water street, Manchester

Cambridge, U.S., Harvard College Library at (per Mr. H. T. Parker)
Campkin, Henry, F.S.A., librarian, Reform club, London, S.W.
Chamberlain, Arthur, Moor Green hall, Moseley, near Birmingham
Chamberlain, John Henry, Christ Church buildings, Birmingham
Christie, Professor, M.A., Owens College, Quay street, Manchester
Cochrane, Alexander, 216, Bath street, Glasgow
Coleridge, Sir J. D. C., M.P., 6, Southwick crescent, London, W.
Collie, John, Alderley Edge, Cheshire
Collier, John Payne, F.S.A., Maidenhead
Cook, Jas. W., 72, Coleman street, City, E.C.
Corser, Rev. Thomas, M.A., F.S.A., Rectory, Stand, near Manchester
Cosens, F. W., Clapham park, London, S.W.
Cowper, J. M., Davington, Faversham
Crossley, James, F.S.A., 2, Cavendish place, Cavendish street, Chorlton-on-Medlock, Manchester, *President*
Croston, James, 6a, St. Ann's square, Manchester

DEVONSHIRE, His Grace the duke of, Devonshire house, Piccadilly, London, W.
Dodds, Rev. James, The Abbey, Paisley, N.B.
Downes, W. W., Bank, Nantwich

ELT, Charles Henry, 1, Noel street, Islington, London, N.
Euing, William, 209, West George street, Glasgow

FAIRBAIRN, Rev. James, Newhaven, Edinburgh
Falconer, Thomas, Usk, Monmouthshire
Feigan, John A., 81, King street, Manchester
Fletcher, John Shepherd, 8, Lever street, Manchester
Forster, John, Palace-gate house, Kensington, London, W.

LIST OF MEMBERS FOR 1870-71.

Fowle, W. F., Boston, U.S. (per Mr. H. T. Parker)
Fry, Danby P., Poor-law Board, Whitehall, London, S.W.
Furnivall, Frederick J., 3, Old square, Lincoln's inn, London, W.C.

GEE, William, High street, Boston, Lincolnshire
Gibbs, Henry H., St. Dunstan's, Regent's park, London, N.W.
Gibbs, William, Tyntesfield, near Bristol
Gratrix, Samuel, 25, Alport town, Deansgate, Manchester
Gray, George, County buildings, Glasgow
Guild, James Wyllie, 3, Park circus, Glasgow

HAILSTONE, Edward, F.S.A., Walton hall, Wakefield, Yorkshire
Halliwell, James Orchard, F.R.S., &c. &c., 6, Tregunter road, London, S.W.
Hamlin, Charles, 27, Virginia street, Glasgow
Hargreaves, George James, Davyhulme, Manchester
Harrison, William, F.S.A., Samlesbury hall, near Preston
Hartford, Connecticut, U.S., Watkinson Library at (per Mr. E. G. Allen)
Hatton, James, Richmond house, Higher Broughton, Manchester
Hayes, Thomas, bookseller, Cross street, Manchester
Haynes, Benjamin, Church park, Mumbles, Swansea
Hayward, Thomas, bookseller, Oxford street, Manchester
Heron, Sir Joseph, knt., Town hall, Manchester
Hewitt, William, Hill side, Fallowfield
Hill, George W., 97, Ingram street, Glasgow
Hopkins, Hugh, 6, Royal Bank place, Glasgow (*Two copies.*)
Howard, Hon. Richard Edward, Stamp office, Manchester, *Treasurer*
Hunt, Edward, chemist, Salford

IRELAND, Alexander, Manchester

JACKSON, H. B., Basford house, Whalley Range, Manchester
Jackson, John, Chancery place, Manchester
Jenner, C., Easter Duddington lodge, Edinburgh
Johnson, Richard, Langton oaks, Fallowfield, Manchester
Jones, Herbert, 1, Church court, Clement's lane, London, E.C.
Jones, Joseph, Abberley hall, Stourport

Jones, Thomas, B.A., F.S.A., Chetham library, Manchester
Jordan, Joseph, F.R.C.S., Bridge street, Manchester.
Jordan, Peter A., 606-614, Sansom street, Philadelphia, U.S.A. (per Trübner and Co., Paternoster row, London, E.C.)

KERSHAW, James, 13, St. Luke's terrace, Cheetham, Manchester
Kershaw, John, Audenshaw, near Manchester
Kershaw, John, Park house, Willesden lane, London, N.W.
King, James, 6, Adelaide place, Glasgow
Knight, Joseph, 27, Camden square, London, N.W.

LANCASHIRE Independent College (per Mr. Joseph Thompson, Pin mill, Ardwick)
Lees, Samuel, junr., Parkbridge, Ashton-under-Lyne
Leigh, Major Egerton, Jodrell hall, near Congleton, Cheshire
Leigh, John, Whalley Range, Manchester
Lembcke, Professor, Marburg (per Williams and Norgate, 14, Henrietta street, Covent garden, London, W.C.)
Lingard, J. R., 12, Booth street, Piccadilly, Manchester
Lingard, R. B. M., 12, Booth street, Piccadilly, Manchester
Lockwood and Co., 7, Stationers' hall court, London, E.C.

McCOWAN, David, 7, Lynedoch crescent, Glasgow
Mackenzie, John Whiteford, 16, Royal circus, Edinburgh
Maclure, John William, Bond street, Manchester
Manchester Free Library, Campfield
Marsden, Rev. Canon, B.D., F.R.S.L., Cliff grange, Higher Broughton, Manchester
Martin, William, city treasurer, Town hall, Manchester
Milne-Redhead, R., Springfield, Seedley, Pendleton, Manchester
Mounsey, G. G., Castletown, near Carlisle
Mountcastle, William, Market street, Manchester
Murdock, James B., 27, Virginia street, Glasgow
Muntz, George H. M., Grosvenor road, Handsworth, Birmingham

NAPIER, George W., 19, Chapel walks, Manchester
Neill, Robert, Northumberland street, Higher Broughton, Manchester

LIST OF MEMBERS FOR 1870-71.

Newcastle-upon-Tyne Literary and Philosophical Society (per Mr. Lyall, librarian)
New York, Clinton Hall Library at (per Sampson Low, Son and Marston, 188, Fleet street, London, E.C.)
Nicholl, George W., The Ham, Cowbridge, Glamorganshire
Nichols George W., Augusta house, Rotherhithe, London, S.E.

OAKEY, John, jun., 172, Blackfriars road, London, S.E.
Owens College Library, Quay street, Manchester
Oxford Union Society (per Mr. Thomas Harris, steward)

PAINE, Cornelius, Oak hill, Surbiton, Surrey
Palin, Captain, Police office, Manchester
Panton, Rev. G. A., 2, Crown circus, Dowanhill, Glasgow
Parker, H. T., 3, Ladbroke gardens, Kensington park, London, W. *(Two Copies.)*
Paterson, William, 74, Princes street, Edinburgh
Paterson, William S., 8, Gordon street, Glasgow
Peace, Maskell W., Green hill, Wigan
Peel, George, Soho foundry, Manchester
Pickering, Basil Montagu, 196, Piccadilly, London, W.
Pocock, C. Innes, Rouge Bouillon, Jersey
Portico Library, Mosley street, Manchester
Priaulx, O. de Beauvoir, 8, Cavendish square, London, W.

QUARITCH, Bernard, 15, Piccadilly, London, W.

REDFERN, Rev. R. S., M.A., Acton vicarage, Nantwich
Reform Club, London, (per Messrs. Ridgway, Piccadilly)
Reynolds, Rev. G. W., Barr hill, Pendleton
Rhodocanakis, H. H. the Prince, Higher Broughton, Manchester
Riggall, Edward, 141, Queen's road, Bayswater, W.
Robinson, Samuel, Black Brook cottage, Wilmslow
Robinson, W. W., New road, Oxford
Ross, Henry, F.S.A., The Manor house, Swanscombe, Kent
Russell, J. R., 1, Stanley place, Paisley road, Glasgow

SAUNDERS, J. Symes, M.D., Devon County Lunatic asylum, Exminster, Exeter
Schofield, Thomas, 1, Apsley terrace, Chester road, Manchester
Scott, James, The Lochies house, Burntisland, N.B.

Sewell, John C., 3, Bridgwater place, High street Manchester
Sharp, John, The Hermitage, near Lancaster
Sheldon, Stephen (per Mr. T. Hayes)
Shields, Thomas, Scarborough
Simms, Charles S., King street, Manchester
Simpson, A. A., Millington Hope, Higher Crump sall, Manchester
Simpson, Joseph, Millington Hope, Higher Crumpsall, Manchester
Simpson, Walter, Bank parade, Preston
Slingluff, C. B., Baltimore (per Mr. B. F. Steven London)
Smith, Alexander, 69, St. George's place, Glasgo
Smith, Fereday, Parkfield, Swinton, Mancheste
Smith, Charles, Faversham, Kent
Snelgrove, Arthur G., London hospital, Londo E.
Sotheby, Mrs. S. Leigh, Leipzig (per Mr. Goo man, 407, Strand, London, W.C.)
Sotheran, Henry, 136, Strand, London, W.C.
Steinthal, H. M., Hollywood, Fallowfield
Stevens, B. F., 17, Henrietta street, Covent garde London, W.C.
Stewart, A. B., 5, Buchanan street, Glasgow
Suthers, Charles, Riversvale, Ashton-under-Lyne
Swindells, George H., Oak villa, Heaton chapel near Stockport

TANNER, Thomas H., M.D., 9, Henrietta street, Cavendish square, London, W.
Taylor, Thomas F., Highfield house, Pemberto Wigan
Thompson, F., South parade, Wakefield
Thompson, Joseph, Pin mill, Ardwick, Manchest
Thorpe, Rev. J. F., Herne hill vicarage, Fave sham, Kent
Timmins, Samuel, F.R.S.L., Elvetham lodge, Bi mingham
Turner, Robert S., 1, Park square, Regent's par London, N.W.

VEITCH, George Seton, 13, Castle terrace, Edinburgh
Vernon, George V., Osborne terrace, Stretfo road, Manchester
Vienna, Imperial Library at (per Asher and C 13, Bedford street, Covent garden, Londo W.C.)

WARD, Henry, 158, Cambridge street, Pimlic London, S.W.
Washington, U.S., Library of Congress at (p Mr. E. G. Allen)
Watson, Robert S., 101, Pilgrim street, Newcast on-Tyne

LIST OF MEMBERS FOR 1870-71.

Weston, George, 2, Gray's inn square, London, W.C.
Weymouth, R. F., D.Lit., Mill Hill school, London, N.W.
Wheatley, H. B., 53, Berners street, London, W.
Whitehead, Jeffery, Barfield lodge, Bickley, Kent
Wilbraham, Henry, Chancery office, Manchester
Woolcombe, Rev. W. W., M.A., Ardwick, Manchester
Wylie, Charles, 3, Earl's terrace, Kensington, London, W.

YOUNG, Alexander, 9, Lynedock place, Glasgow
Young, George, 9, Lynedock place, Glasgow

www.ingramcontent.com/pod-product-compliance
Lightning Source LLC
Chambersburg PA
CBHW031329230426
43670CB00006B/290